Community Living Skills

**Monographs of the
American Association on Mental Retardation, 10**

Michael J. Begab, Series Editor

Community Living Skills

A
Taxonomy

by

R. B. Dever
Indiana University

with a chapter by

Dennis R. Knapczyk
Indiana University

Published by
American Association on Mental Retardation
1719 Kalorama Road, NW
Washington, DC 20009

No. 10, Monographs of the American Association on Mental Retardation (ISSN 0895-8009)

Preparation of this manuscript was partially supported by Grant No. USDE G008430112 from the U.S. Office of Special Education and Rehabilitation Services, and by a grant from the Governor's Council on Developmental Disabilities in the State of Indiana. The author was encouraged to express his opinions freely. Points of view herein do not neccessarily represent the policies or opinions of the funding agencies.

Library of Congress Cataloging-in-Publication Data

Dever, R. B. (Richard Bernard), 1934–
    Community living skills.

    (Monographs of the American Association on Mental Retardation ; 10)
    Bibliography: p.
    Includes index.
    1. Mentally handicapped—United States—Life skills guides—Outlines, syl-
labi, etc. 2. Life skills—Study and teaching—United States—Handbooks, manuals,
etc. 3. Mentally handicapped—Deinstitutionalization—Handbooks, manuals, etc.
4. Mentally handicapped—Education—Handbooks, manuals, etc. 5. Community
education—United States—Curricula. I. Knapczyk, Dennis R. II. American Association on Mental Retardation. III. Title. IV. Series.

HV3004.D48   1988   362.3′8   88-943
ISBN 0-940898-19-5 (pbk.)

Printed in the United States of America

Contents

Contents

The purpose of this taxonomy is to provide a complete statement of the goals of community-based instruction. It should prove useful to those who develop curricula in community agencies that have instructional programs for persons who have difficulty living in the community without assistance. These agencies would include not only the public schools, but also rehabilitation agencies, alternative living facilities, and other agencies established to help people take control over their own lives.

In the final analysis, the *Community Living Skills* taxonomy is a career education document: it specifies instructional goals for curricula that can begin at infancy and end at the point at which learners take their places in the community. Basically, it provides a template to place on the local community to assist curriculum developers in understanding what they should look for when making decisions about what to teach. Once the endpoints are clear, it will become possible to develop curriculum pathways toward those goals.

By itself, the taxonomy is not a curriculum: it does not include everything that low-functioning learners must learn. On the contrary, it provides *only* the endpoints of instruction in community living skills. Because skill performance varies from place to place, the curricula leading to those endpoints will have to be constructed by local agencies, that is, local people will have to discover how the endpoints are realized in their communities and develop their own instructional paths leading to those endpoints.

It is necessary to point out that learners may also participate in instructional programs leading to other goals. For example, a physically handicapped intellectually normal learner who is being taught to maintain his own living quarters may also participate in a curriculum designed to train people to do technical or professional work. Nevertheless, despite the fact that the scope of the goal statement in this manual is actually quite limited, it should be of great use to those who must develop curricula for community living skills.

The taxonomy took nearly seven years to complete, and a large number of persons were involved in the development of the ideas. These persons were found in various capacities and locations and they worked hard in developing the foundation for the taxonomy. During this period, there were times when I was the only one who had any idea of where events were leading: especially in the early years, I was often unable to state that point with sufficient clarity to enable people to understand what was supposed to happen. Nevertheless, they hung in there, and without their insights it would never have been possible to complete the work. I thank them for their patience and perseverence in the face of what must often have seemed like nonsense. They are:

MUSCATATUCK DEVELOPMENTAL CENTER STAFF
BUTLERVILLE, INDIANA

Dennis Barrett	Cathy Grigsby	Sue Renfro
Charles Chambers	Glenn Heath	Dolores Sanders
Patricia Cook	Mark Jarman	Linda Steffey
Jerry Craddock	William Kelly	Geralann Straub
George Duffitt	Betty Leahigh	Christy Swango
Kay Fox	Evelyn Niemeyer	Mary Tate
Carlotta Garwood	Alberta T. Phillips	Michael Wallace
Ruth Gholson	Janet Proctor	Nina Ward
Pauline Gregory		

DEVELOPMENTAL SERVICES, INC., STAFF
COLUMBUS, INDIANA

Mary Austin	Nancy Pulley	Kathleen Vogler
Rita Coyle	Steven Savage	

BARTHOLOMEW COUNTY
SPECIAL SERVICES CORPORATION STAFF
COLUMBUS, INDIANA

Sandra Allen	David Johnson	Shirley Trapp
Emily Baker	Kathleen Knight	Herschel Willey
Debra Goens		

MONROE COUNTY COMMUNITY SCHOOLS
CORPORATION STAFF
BLOOMINGTON, INDIANA

Sean Hammond	Maxine Prather

INDIANA UNIVERSITY SEMINAR GROUPS

Scott Boleman
Marianne Caprino
Carol Detmer
Susan Fischel
Mark Girt
Diana Hymen

Theresa Kindred
Susan Larmore
Beresford Jones
Mary Marlowe
Charles McGary
Debra Moore

Linda Reed
Georgia Sherriff
Becky Siefer
Laura Stachowsky

Richard B. Dever
Indiana University
January, 1988

Section I

**Organization
and
Use of the
_____Taxonomy**

Chapter 1
Introduction

BACKGROUND

Until 1957, the term *taxonomy* was used almost exclusively by life scientists to refer to the various classification schemes for categorizing the biological world. The application of the term to classifications of instructional goals and objectives began with what is known as the "Bloom Taxonomy" (Bloom, 1956).[1] That document focused largely on classifying the cognitive objectives of American general public education, but recognized the importance of motor and social objectives as well. It has been used as a guide by American educators ever since its publication.

The taxonomy in this manual attempts to accomplish something different from the Bloom taxonomy, i.e., it classifies skills required for daily life in the community. It focuses not on the objectives of general education, but rather on the instructional goals for a specific group of learners—those who have difficulty learning to become functioning members of a community. It was designed to assist in the process of curriculum development for these persons.

A taxonomy does not constitute a curriculum: this manual contains only a statement of the endpoints of instruction in community living. It does not attempt to provide curricula leading to those endpoints. As a result, many of the skills the reader may expect to find in a curriculum are not present in this document. For example, no mention is made of *language, motor,* or *academic* skills. Instruction in these topics would fall into the category of *prerequisites* or *precursors* to many of the goals in this manual and are not properly listed as goals per se.

The taxonomic system presented here evolved over a long period. The effort began in 1980 when the author was assigned the task of developing a curriculum for a residential facility in Indiana (Dever, 1983). The original intent was to adapt existing curricula and work out a kind of curriculum pastiche that could be used to guide the instructional programs of the facility's learners. After two years of searching through various curricula, however, the conclusion was reached that nothing in print provided what was needed. The basic problem was that the curricula surveyed did not seem to have any particular point; most of the curricula inspected seemed to consist of collections of items designed merely to bring learners "up to

---

[1] The "Bloom Taxonomy" was actually the product of a committee established by the American Educational Research Association that was chaired by Dr. Bloom.

zero," or the point at which they could begin to learn to do important things (Gold, 1980). The goals of instruction either were not present or were difficult to discern in these documents. Some curricula did specify goals clearly, but they were usually too constrained in scope to govern instruction for the facility; that is, they dealt with specific topics such as language, or motor skills. Consequently, late in 1981 the decision was made to develop a curriculum independently. By this time, the definitions presented in Chapter 2 had been developed, and the project that eventually produced the taxonomy was able to get underway in earnest.

USE OF THE TAXONOMY

The need to develop a taxonomy of community living skills grew out of the author's work with persons who have moderate, severe, and profound mental retardation in both public schools and adult service agencies. The use of this manual is probably wider than this statement would suggest, however, because retarded persons are not the only ones who experience difficulty in learning to live in the community: other groups also have this problem (e.g., less seriously retarded groups, groups with physical or sensory disabilities, released prisoners, and many immigrant [and other non-English-speaking populations] as well). Workers who are in a position to develop programs of instruction in community living for any of these groups should find the taxonomy useful.

The age range of the learners who can benefit from curricula that lead to the goals in this manual is very large. That is, community living skills must be learned by some groups of adults as well as by school children. Therefore, not only will public schools find this taxonomy useful, but so also will certain adult service agencies, e.g., rehabilitation centers for handicapped adults and agencies with community living programs such as group homes and halfway houses.

Two groups of professionals in particular will find this taxonomy useful: administrators in instructional service facilities such as public schools, rehabilitation centers, group homes, and supported employment agencies; and curriculum developers.

Administrators

Although the taxonomy was created to provide a guide for curriculum developers, the clearly stated instructional goals provide administrators with a tool not previously available. This tool can be used in various ways.

Clarifying Program Thrust

The most efficient programs are those that have a sharp focus upon which everyone agrees. Unfortunately, many agencies allow programs to spring up "like Topsy," perhaps for economic reasons: a notice for a potential grant appears in the mail, and because it sounds like a good idea, a proposal is submitted. In a short time, the agency has a melange of programs and everyone seems to be going off in different directions. In contrast, the agency that clearly understands the purpose of its programs and the direction in which it should go will be able to focus both its programs and its search for funding.

A second reason for agencies to develop a clear idea of program thrust is to increase the efficiency of individual programs within the agency. Administrators must review program thrusts periodically because the boundaries of agency activities tend to become blurred over time. For example, community living programs (such as group home programs) often try to teach academic skills; public school programs often try to teach home living skills; and vocational programs often try to teach leisure skills. In each case, a more focused program would be more appropriate. The goals listed in this taxonomy can help administrators clarify program thrust. Each major goal should be considered with the following question in mind: *Should one or more of the agency's programs be trying to help people attain this goal, or is it best left to another program or agency?* Periodic reviews of an agency's programs relative to the instructional goals listed in this manual will help to keep the programs on track.

Conducting Curriculum Projects

A third major activity for all agencies serving persons who require instruction is curriculum development. Each agency must construct its own curricula for two reasons:

1. Communities vary greatly from one to another, and a curriculum constructed for one community may not be useful in a different one. For instance, nearly everyone must learn to travel about his or her community in order to be independent. Such travel will take a number of different forms depending on the community in which it is to take place. For example, public transportation is readily available in some places, while in many it is not. This fact alone means that a single curriculum for all communities could not be constructed. In addition, even the communities that have public transportation systems have very different facilities: learning to travel around Chicago is quite different from learning to travel around Bloomington, Indiana, Los Angeles, California, or Quincy, Massachusetts.

2. The second reason for each agency to construct its own curricula is that agencies with different thrusts serve persons at different age levels and at different levels of functioning. Consequently, agency populations, missions, and programs are so varied that a single curriculum could not be created to serve them all. Therefore, public schools must construct curricula for some skills, rehabilitation centers

must construct curricula for other skills, and group homes must construct still others for other skills. Only when different agencies are working toward the same goal skills will they be able to construct curricula they can share.

Curriculum development has often meant a rehashing of existing work. Unfortunately, as many workers have stated (Guess et al., 1978; Haring 1977b), most existing curricula are very limited, and new ones will have to be constructed. Because this manual specifies instructional goals clearly, curriculum development teams will find their work easier to define.

The manual will help in the following ways:

1. It will be possible to assign tasks and deadlines to the various personnel involved in the curriculum project. The existence of sharply defined instructional goals provides a clarity of focus not previously available, and allows administrators to set forth clearcut tasks for the personnel involved in curriculum construction.

2. Because the taxonomy provides benchmarks for completion of the task, it allows the administrator to decide whether the curriculum has been completed or whether there is still work to do.

Curriculum Developers

This taxonomy was constructed primarily to assist in curriculum development. Those who become involved in curriculum construction projects will find this taxonomy useful in several ways. Chief among them will be the assistance the manual can provide in clarifying the parameters of the task of the curriculum development team.

Defining Parameters

Like administrators, curriculum development teams must define the parameters within which they will carry out their functions prior to engaging in their activities. When an individual or group sets out to construct a curriculum, the first step is to decide what the curriculum will be *for*. Questions such as the following will help clarify the task: Should the curriculum attempt to teach learners to take care of a home setting, or should it try to teach them to perform jobs? Should it try to do both? If questions similar to these are answered at the start of the venture, the task will be clear and the chances of success will be increased: a curriculum development group that begins its task with a close consideration of the goal statements in an effort to define the outcomes of the curriculum will be more likely to complete the task than one that does not.

Because the goals are clearly stated, much of the fuzziness of the task of constructing curricula will be eliminated for the project participants and much of the "circle, square, and triangle" type of curricula will no longer be necessary. Instead, agency personnel can now focus on the skills learners need to be more independent and find curricular pathways to those skills.

Once the goals of the future curriculum have been decided upon, the development team must begin finding curricular pathways to those goals. The specific content of those paths will be idiosyncratic because there is no single way to reach a goal. Some techniques for constructing those pathways are presented in Knapczyk's discussion (Chapter 4).

Community Surveys

A major activity of curriculum developers when they construct community-based curricula is to survey the environment to find out what the learners will have to do at the end of instruction. It is one thing to say that learners must learn how to buy groceries and another to say that they must learn to buy groceries in the local Stop and Buylow store (or whatever supermarket is available). Community surveys of the goal behaviors will provide the kind of detail that is required (Brown et al., 1980). Given a clear statement of goals, it will be easier to ascertain what to look for when the time comes to investigate the community.

CONCLUDING STATEMENT

Many persons will find this taxonomy useful. Administrators and curriculum developers will be the primary user groups, but those who have a stake in the advancement of learners should find this manual of assistance to them in their work. A major use will be to clarify the perceptions of those who are in positions to influence instruction in one way or another. Those who believe that instruction should lead toward increased independence for learners will find that this taxonomy provides a set of very clear statements as to what they must be able to do.

The taxonomy provides the completed first step in developing curricula within the parameters of the instructional paradigm (see Chapter 2). The project in which it was developed had but a single goal: to state clearly the skills that people have to exhibit in a community without attracting negative attention and without requiring supervision.

The curricula that might be constructed under the aegis of the taxonomy vary enormously. A vocational training center, for example, might not want to stray beyond the boundaries established for the Vocational Domain, while a public school program serving a wide range of handicapped persons might try to construct a broader curriculum. Another agency serving only preschool-aged children would focus its curricula exclusively on the early developing prerequisite and precursor skills that lead to the goals (but would not try to teach the goals themselves), while an agency serving mildly handicapped adults might focus on teaching skills just as they are listed in the taxonomy. In all cases, the taxonomy provides a set of benchmarks for the construction of curricula appropriate to the needs of both learners and agencies.

Chapter 2

Parameters of
_____the Taxonomy

For many years curriculum theorists have insisted that the first step in building curricula is to establish the goals of instruction (Dewey, 1902; Popham & Baker, 1970; Smith, Stanley, & Shores, 1957; Taba, 1962; Tanner & Tanner, 1980; Tyler, 1957). It is interesting to note, however, that few curricula for disabled persons have been constructed in this manner. The major exceptions are found in the work of those espousing career education (e.g., Kokaska & Brolin, 1986), or in extremely limited areas of instruction such as motor skills or language (e.g., Dever, 1978).

The taxonomy in this manual grew out of a conviction that instruction must be focused to be effective. It was developed within the parameters of the _instructional paradigm_, which requires all instruction to begin with a consideration of goals. John Dewey once stated it as follows:

> To see the outcome is to know in what direction the present experience is moving . . . The far-away point, which is of no significance to us simply as far-away, becomes of huge importance the moment we take it as defining a present direction of movement . . . it is no remote and distant result to be achieved, but a guiding method in dealing with the present." (Dewey, 1902, p. 18)

In other words, the instructional paradigm holds that only when the ends of instruction are made clear will it become possible to find curricular paths to those goals.

Therefore, in order to develop curricula within its parameters, the first step is to develop a list of the goals toward which the curricula will lead. That first step is represented by this taxonomy. _Community Living Skills_ incorporates the instructional paradigm as a system of thought, and presents a coherent statement of instructional goals that curriculum developers can use to define the direction of their curricula. The goals can serve both as templates to place on the community to discover specific skills that members of the community must exhibit, and as a set of benchmarks for the curricula that must be constructed for specific agencies.

THE INSTRUCTIONAL
PARADIGM

The instructional paradigm produces the classic methodology for constructing curricula; that is, it first tries to understand important instructional goals and then constructs curricula leading toward those goals. These curricula, in turn, can be used to develop individual programs of instruction.

The instructional paradigm does not attend to any individual's degree of disability. That is, while it is an unfortunate fact that certain individuals can never attain the goals stated in this manual because their physical or intellectual deficits are so great, the goals cannot change. The primary purpose of this taxonomy is to present instructional goals that will make it possible to work out curricular pathways to those goals. The guiding principle is that the goals must respond to a general need that can be addressed by curricula. If the work is done well, the beginning of the instructional pathways toward the goals will provide the content of the instructional program for young or very low-functioning persons. Until the ends of instruction are clearly identified, however, finding the beginnings will not be possible. Although this view may not reflect the predominant view in the field of disabilities in recent years, it clearly holds promise for the eventual construction of good curricula that can be used to provide instruction to a very wide range of persons.

Actions In the Instructional Paradigm

A schematic diagram of action within the context of the instructional paradigm is presented in Figure 2-1. The steps that must be taken to teach are as follows.

Establish the Aim of Instruction

The first step is to establish the aim of instruction: what instruction intends to accomplish if it is successful. For example, the decision might be made to train learners to be artists, or plumbers, or politicians (among many other things). For the purposes of this taxonomy, the aim of instruction is to teach learners to live in the community without extraordinary supervision. (This statement is extended and clarified in the definition of independence presented later in this chapter.)

Set the Goals of Instruction

The second step is to establish goals of instruction that are consistent with the aim. In doing so, the idea is to specify in some detail the skills the learner is expected to exhibit by the time instruction is complete. For exam-

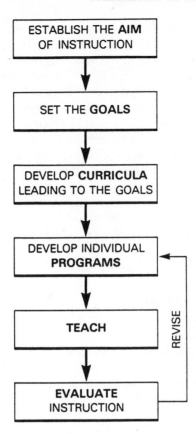

FIGURE 2-1: The Instructional Paradigm.

ple, instruction might aim to teach learners to apply the Theory of Relativity in astronomical experiments, or it might aim to teach learners to produce leak-free welds on oil pipelines. For the purposes of this taxonomy, the goals of instruction consist of the specific skills required to live unsupervised in the community.

Develop Curricula Leading to the Goals

A curriculum is a set of instructional pathways to a goal or a set of goals. Only after the goals of instruction are clearly established does it become possible to construct curricula that lead to them. Thus, within the parameters of the instructional paradigm, a curriculum can be seen as analogous to planning a trip—that is, once the traveler knows the destination, he or she can find a way to get there; however, if the traveler does not know where he or she is going, getting there is impossible. Similarly, if the goals of instruction are clear it is possible to construct a curriculum; if they are not, it is impossible to find "a way to get there."

Interestingly, different groups working to construct curricula leading to the same goals might develop quite different curricula, all of which could be valid. An example of such a case is easy to find. For example, two groups might construct curricula to teach severely handicapped persons to perform jobs (a goal in the Vocational Domain). Both groups may succeed, but they can do so in very different ways: some groups have developed industries that are completely (or almost completely) staffed by severely disabled persons, while others have developed systems for training severely disabled persons to perform ordinary service jobs in the community (Vash, 1977). The end result in each case is that severely disabled persons learn to do jobs that are needed by society and that remunerate workers appropriately for their efforts. Note that both sets of curricula lead toward the same goal, and that each can provide useful instruction. Which curriculum is "better" is a matter for individual communities to define.

Develop Individual Programs

Once the curricula are constructed, it becomes possible to assess individual learners to discover how much they already know and how much they have yet to learn. Few learners enter an instructional setting knowing nothing at all: rather, nearly all have some skills. The problem for programmers is to discover learner performance characteristics: how many of the target skills does each learner have now, and how many does he or she yet have to learn? Answers to these questions will provide information that can be used to develop individual programs of instruction and will determine the form an individual program should take.

Teach

Once the programs have been developed, the next step is to teach. This statement requires few explanations, except to say that, under the instructional paradigm, the learner should move as quickly and as far as possible toward the goals. In this view, the act of teaching requires that decisions be made on how the information should be presented, how motivation should be maintained, and how skills should be generalized and maintained after the learner acquires them.

Evaluate Instruction

The end of the cycle requires that the instruction be evaluated. If all of the other steps have been carried out well, this step is easy to accomplish because the instructional personnel will have a very clear idea of what the learner is supposed to be learning and appropriate criteria for discovering whether or not progress is being made. If the learner is progressing appropriately, instruction should continue as planned in the program; if not, changes must be made in either the program or the instructional techniques or both.

APPLYING THE INSTRUCTIONAL
PARADIGM

The instructional paradigm is not universally accepted by those who work with disabled persons despite the fact that the need for instruction has been noted many times. For example, one of the groups that has worked the longest for the benefit of persons with disabilities is the American Association on Mental Retardation (AAMR). In the century since it was formed, workers in the field have returned again and again to the idea that the basic problem facing persons who are mentally retarded is their need for instruction (Sarason & Doris, 1969; Scheerenberger, 1983). Indeed, for the last quarter of a century, each of the manuals on definition and classification of mental retardation published by the AAMR (Grossman, 1973, 1983; Heber, 1962) has stated that retarded persons who learn to exhibit enough skills *(adaptive behaviors)* can no longer be called retarded. This statement implies that instruction could ameliorate mental retardation. Despite such strong statements, however, there has never been a nationally agreed upon set of instructional goals for the retarded or for any group of severely disabled persons. This is not to say that no attempts have been made to develop such statements. On the contrary, those who have adopted a career education perspective have been working at the task for a long time (e.g., Brolin, 1978; Kokaska & Brolin, 1986). Nevertheless, there is no national consensus on the goals of instruction at the time of this writing.

The Aim of Instruction

Because the taxonomy was constructed under the classical assumption that it is necessary to know exactly what to teach before beginning to teach it, the first step in its construction was to specify its aim, or what should result from instruction if it is successful. By extension, the aim of the taxonomy will also be the aim of any curricula developed under its aegis.

Independence is commonly seen as the aim of instruction for persons with disabilities. Unfortunately, it is an elusive concept: although many of us think of ourselves as independent, to a large degree we are very much dependent on others (and they are dependent on us). For example, we rely on other people to bring food to the supermarkets, cart away our garbage, fix our automobiles, put out fires, and keep track of our bank accounts, to list just a few things. Clearly, teaching people to be *independent* does not mean that we should teach them totally to lack dependence: if the concept of independence is to be at all useful, it must be clarified in such a manner that it can be used to guide instruction.

An earlier paper presented a version of the definition of *independence* under which all work on the taxonomy was carried out. It is as follows:

> *Independence* is exhibiting behavior patterns appropriate to the behavior settings that are normally frequented by others of the individual's age and social status in such a manner that the individual is not perceived as requiring supervision because of his behavior. (Dever, 1983)

Under this definition, the term independence now provides a clear aim for the taxonomy and for any curricula subsequently developed under its guidance. In colloquial terms, it says that learners with disabilities must be taught to go where other people go, do what they do there, and not look different because of the way they do it.

This definition relies on the concepts of *behavior pattern* and *behavior setting* as set forth by Roger Barker (1968). Briefly, these terms refer to the fact that human behavior is largely determined by the setting in which the person is located; in fact, the behavior of an individual in any behavior setting is far more similar to that of other people in the setting than it is to the behavior of the same person across different settings.

Behavior settings literally determine the behaviors we are allowed to exhibit. For example, anyone who goes to the supermarket must do the things that people do in supermarkets; similarly, anyone who goes to church must do the things that people do in church. If, however, anyone should go to the supermarket and there do the things that people do in church, the consequences would be immediate, negative, and severe.

In other words, the definition leads to the conclusion that persons who cannot now live unsupervised must be taught to depend on other persons in the usual manner as well as to be dependable themselves; that is, to do things in such a way that they become part of the fabric of the community.[2] With this aim to guide the project, the work of developing this taxonomy required that daily life be analyzed, catalogued, and organized in such a way that the information could be used for instructional purposes.

Curriculum Versus Program

There seems to be some confusion in the literature between the terms *curriculum* and *program*. These terms require differentiation and clarification if the taxonomy is to be useful.

---

[2] This thought was suggested by Dr. Joseph Koonz (private communication). It is very subtle, and very powerful in its potential impact.

A curriculum is the set of skills that anyone would have to learn in order to attain an instructional goal or set of goals. A program, as set forth in the rules emanating from PL 94-142 and Section 504 of the Amendments to the Rehabilitation Act of 1973, is the set of tasks and skills that will be the focus of a specific learner's instruction during a specified period of time (Haring, 1977b). In other words, whereas a curriculum attends to the content of instruction per se (the *what* and *why* of instruction) and ignores individuals, a program details the specific curricular content that an individual will be taught under a specified set of circumstances (the *who, when, where*, and *how* of instruction).

Goals Versus Objectives

The taxonomy lists instructional goals—or the end points of instruction. The term *goal* has multiple meanings, however, because there is more than one end point of instruction. That is, both a curriculum and a program have goals, but they are not usually identical. For example, an individual program plan (abbreviated IEP, IPP, IHP, IRP, ITP, etc., by different groups of professionals) must contain a list of the goals the learner will attain prior to the time the next program plan is to be developed (Haring, 1977a). Such goals are always supposed to be attainable by the individual in the near future, for example, in 6–12 months. A curriculum goal, on the other hand, is quite different, because it is not a goal for an individual—rather, it is the end point of a curricular pathway. Realistically, it may be many years before some individuals will be able to attain some curriculum goals, and, sadly, some individuals may never attain many curriculum goals in their lifetimes (although they may attain a number of program goals).[3]

A similar distinction must be made between a curriculum objective and a program objective. That is, although the term *objective* can be thought of as consisting of a step toward a goal in both instances, there are differences between an objective in a program plan (a step toward a program goal) and an objective in a curriculum (a step toward a curriculum goal). Note that a curriculum objective may, in fact, become a program goal; it could be made a thrust of the learner's program. The reverse is not true, however: a

---

[3] The fact that some persons may never reach the goals of a curriculum does not negate the goals. It simply means that some people cannot go all the way through the curriculum. It is not unusual for such a thing to happen because many people (the author among them) have entered curricula they could not complete, such as those constructed for developing theoretical mathematicians. The fact that some people can go only partway through certain curricula, as illustrated by this example, does not mean that there is no point in entering them. For example, although I never became a mathematician, I can balance my checkbook, figure the number of board feet in a stack of lumber, and calculate how long it will take to drive from Indiana to Connecticut. Obviously, partial progress through a curriculum can have its benefits.

program objective can never become a curriculum goal because, in the instructional paradigm, the curriculum exists prior to the program.

CONCLUDING STATEMENT

Community Living Skills has the limited purpose of listing the goals for curricula that teach individuals how to live in the community. It does not attempt to provide program goals for any individual, nor does it attempt to provide the curricula from which program goals could be derived. Developing such curricula would be the next step, according to the instructional paradigm, and it is properly left to various agencies in the communities to be carried out.

Every goal that people might seek has not been listed in the taxonomy. On the contrary, a learner who can do everything he or she needs to live unsupervised in the community may also be ready to enroll in other curricula that have other goals. For example, a person who learns to exhibit a large number of the skills contained in this manual may be ready to go to the local community college to learn a trade that pays more than his or her current job, or to go to cooking classes to learn Cajun cooking (or whatever). The point is that this taxonomy covers only the basic skills required for community living. Curricula developed under its aegis may not provide the only instruction for an individual. Because many people who live in the community participate in other curricula, there is no reason to believe that persons with disabilities could not do likewise if they can learn to live in the community without supervision.

The instructional paradigm is a useful tool for those who must teach. It is older than civilization in that it dates all the way back to the time when the first elders began to teach their young to gather food, clothe their bodies, and appease the gods. *Community Living Skills* represents an attempt to apply this paradigm to the instruction of persons with disabilities and to bring the concept of instruction into sharp focus in the field.

Chapter 3

Organization
of the
Taxonomy

During the developmental period, various organizational schemes were considered for use in the taxonomy. A survey of curriculum guides revealed that some had as many as 12 categories of instructional items (e.g., East Allen Public Schools, n.d.), while others had as few as four (e.g., Gunzburg, 1973; Sailor, 1975). Although many of the curricula surveyed contained elements of the organization used in this manual in one form or another, the organization used here is slightly different from all of them.

Organizations are neither good nor bad, right nor wrong: they can only be useful or not useful. Like any organization, the one used in this taxonomy was imposed and arbitrary. Therefore, the precise classification of some goals might be seen differently by different persons. This fact should not present a problem if the reader keeps in mind the arbitrary nature of organizations. The one used in this manual can help in the following ways:

1. The taxonomic model generally corresponds to the manner in which persons differentiate activities in their daily lives. Although some persons are bound to disagree about the classification of specific skills (because of variations in individual perceptions), a national survey conducted during the developmental phase of the project indicated that the model is generally acceptable to workers in the field.

2. The model generally reflects the manner in which the distinction between mission and service is made within agencies that serve disabled persons.

3. The model provides a mnemonic system that is easy to remember and will help curriculum development teams to stay organized.

Taken together, the organization used to classify skills thus seems useful. The model and the manner in which the taxonomy was developed are the subjects of this chapter.

THE FIVE DOMAINS

The taxonomic model is presented in Figure 3-1. The five domains within which the goals are organized are as follows.

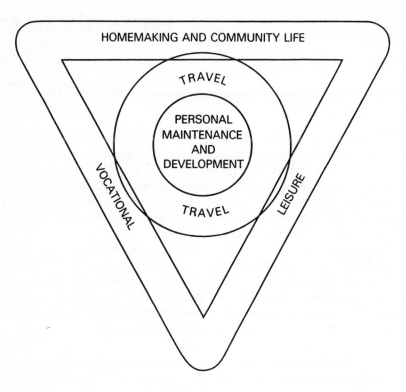

FIGURE 3-1: Organization of the Taxonomy.

Personal Maintenance and Development Domain

This domain contains the skills an individual must exhibit in order to maintain himself or herself personally. This category includes not only the traditional self-help skills such as washing, toileting, and grooming, but also the skills necessary to establish and maintain good relationships with family and friends, and those required to cope with life's daily "glitches,"[4] or manifestations of Murphy's Law.[5]

Homemaking and Community Life Domain

This domain contains the skills involved in finding and maintaining living quarters, budgeting money, and maintaining nutrition. It also contains the skills required to establish and maintain good relationships with neighbors, local merchants, and community officials of one kind or another (such as policemen). This domain also contains the skills required to cope with the glitches found in community daily life.

Vocational Domain

This domain is concerned with the world of work. It contains the skills involved in finding a job, performing the work, and using the worksite. It also contains the skills required for establishing and maintaining good relationships with the boss and fellow workers, and for coping with the glitches found in the workplace.

Leisure Domain

This is the "time off" domain: it is concerned with the skills exhibited when the person is not working, taking care of himself, or maintaining his living quarters. It focuses on matters such as learning new leisure activities, selecting activities from the range available, and performing the desired activities in an effective manner. It is also concerned with developing and maintaining good interpersonal relationships during leisure activities and with coping with the glitches encountered while at leisure.

---

[4] The closest thing to an original contribution in the taxonomy is the category of "glitches" that appears in each domain. The idea is not completely new, however: Dr. Robert Zuckerman, at Kent State University, informs me that he worked with the concept under the head of *common sense*, especially as it refers to *unanticipated events*. Others have suggested that the concept has appeared under headings such as *adaptability, potential errors,* and *exceptions*. Although there is every reason to believe these statements, the fact remains that the concept has not been in general use.

Some persons have objected to the use of the term *glitches,* as being too slangy. The decision to continue to use it was made because no really good alternative seems to be available. The *Random House Dictionary of English Usage* states that the term derives from a Yiddish word meaning "a minor defect in a machine or plan." As such, it expresses the meaning intended quite well.

[5] Murphy's Law states: "If anything can go wrong, it will." Murphy's Law is well developed, and now has thousands of corollaries, such as "Dropped toast always lands jelly-side down." It is also nondiscriminative—it applies equally to all, regardless of race, creed, sex, age, or national origin.

Travel Domain

This domain contains the skills required for moving about the community. It is concerned both with the use of conveyances and the development of "mental maps" of the various environments found in the community. The Travel Domain also contains the skills required for developing and maintaining good interpersonal relationships during travel, and for coping with the glitches found during travel.

The diagram in Figure 3-1 shows a measure of overlap across domains. Although each domain is independent of the others in all *major* respects, human experience does not always lend itself to being classified in neat little boxes. For example, the Vocational Domain and the Homemaking and Community Life Domain are independent of one another; however, the fact that one generally wears one's workclothes at work and cleans them at home creates a degree of overlap between them. Similarly, the Travel and Leisure Domains are independent, but because travel per se can constitute a leisure activity for some people, there is a degree of overlap. Accordingly, the diagram in Figure 3-1 indicates no clear separation between any of the domains.

Note that three of the domains focus on life in the community: Homemaking and Community Life, Leisure, and Vocational. These domains are represented as forming a triangle, with the tips connecting to indicate the overlap. These three domains surround the person (indicated by the circle at the center of the diagram), just as the community surrounds the person in life. Connecting the person with the community is the circle representing the Travel Domain, which is comprised of skills that allow the person to move through his environment. Thus, the pictorial representation of the organization of the taxonomy is mnemonic.

Contents of the Domains

Table 3-1 contains a list of the major goals found in the taxonomy. Inspection of this list shows that the content of three domains—Homemaking and Community Life, Leisure, and Vocational—are parallel in structure. Each contains sections on discovering the environment, performing routines, handling interpersonal relationships, and coping with glitches. However, two domains (Personal Maintenance and Development, and Travel) do not contain sections relating to discovering the environment because discovery is not pertinent to these domains. For example, in the Personal Maintenance and Development Domain, the person himself is a given, that is, people do not have to locate themselves in the same sense that they must locate a job or a place to live. Similarly, travel is a given in that it begins as soon as the person notices something outside himself or herself. Therefore, finding travel is also not a problem. These two domains, then, do not have initial sections parallel to those of the other three.

Glitches

The idea of including glitches developed when one of the groups involved in the project began to be concerned with the fact that retarded persons are usually taught to go through a day that has no problems. That is, even though daily life is full of minor problems with which everyone must learn to cope, persons with disabilities are often shielded from experiencing them. From the learner's point of view, the day usually tends to go very smoothly: at 9:00 a.m. Activity A happens, at 9:45 Activity B happens, and at 10:45 everyone moves off to engage in Activity C. Although problems arise during the day, most are solved by staff and the learner rarely has to deal with them.

In the real world, however, Murphy's Law reigns. There are times when the first thing that happens when we wake up is that we break a shoelace; then we discover that we forgot to buy milk the day before and now we must do without our morning cereal, and by the time we get through coping with these events, we discover that we have missed the bus and that we will be late for work, etc. Some days are worse than others; sometimes it seems that just being able to sleep all day would be an "upper." If real life has such days, it is necessary to teach learners not only that things can and do go wrong, but also that it is possible to cope with the problems that arise. Those who do not learn to cope with such problems will not be able to live without supervision. Hence, the inclusion of the category of glitches.

In general, glitches seem to fall into one of three categories: breakdowns of tools or equipment (e.g., shoelaces that break); depletions of materials (e.g., milk that runs out); and (c) schedule problems (e.g., being late for work). All three types of problems are present in each of the five domains.

Potential Confusion

There is a possibility that too much rationalization about the classification of specific skills can cause confusion. For example, the tasks performed while taking care of oneself are different from those performed while caring for one's living quarters, performing a job, or engaging in leisure or travel tasks. However, some people may have to cook food at work as well as at home (e.g., short order cooks) and some others may find tasks such as mowing the grass to be a pleasant leisure activity. In other words, the lines between domains can become blurred at times because of circumstances, and it would be easy to quibble with the classifications of nearly any skill. In fact, during the development of the taxonomy, discussion would sometimes become completely bogged down in details of this nature. Eventually, the decision was made to use what was seen as the purest case whenever there might be a question as to where a skill belonged in the taxonomy. It is necessary, therefore, to remember that any classification scheme results from a set of arbitrary decisions; those made for this taxonomy should be seen simply for what they are.

TABLE 3-1

Taxonomy of Community Living Skills
(List of Major Goals)

DOMAIN P: Personal Maintenance and Development

I. *The learner will follow routine body maintenance procedures*
   A. Maintain personal cleanliness
   B. Groom self
   C. Dress appropriately
   D. Follow appropriate sleep patterns
   E. Maintain nutrition
   F. Exercise regularly
   G. Maintain substance control

II. *The learner will treat illnesses*
   A. Use first aid and illness treatment procedures
   B. Obtain medical advice when necessary
   C. Follow required medication schedules

III. *The learner will establish and maintain personal relationships*
   A. Interact appropriately with family
   B. Make friends
   C. Interact appropriately with friends
   D. Cope with inappropriate conduct of family and friends
   E. Respond to sexual needs
   F. Obtain assistance in maintaining personal relationships

IV. *The learner will handle personal glitches*
   A. Cope with changes in daily schedule
   B. Cope with equipment breakdowns and material depletions

DOMAIN H: Homemaking and Community Life

I. *The learner will obtain living quarters*
   A. Find appropriate living quarters
   B. Rent/buy living quarters
   C. Set up living quarters

II. *The learner will follow community routines*
   A. Keep living quarters neat and clean
   B. Keep fabrics neat and clean
   C. Maintain interior of living quarters
   D. Maintain exterior of living quarters
   E. Respond to seasonal changes
   F. Follow home safety procedures
   G. Follow accident/emergency procedures
   H. Maintain foodstock
   I. Prepare and serve meals
   J. Budget money appropriately
   K. Pay bills

III. *The learner will coexist in a neighborhood and community*
   A. Interact appropriately with community members
   B. Cope with inappropriate conduct of others
   C. Observe requirements of the law
   D. Carry out civic duties

IV. *The learner will handle glitches in the home*
   A. Cope with equipment breakdowns
   B. Cope with depletions of household supplies
   C. Cope with unexpected depletions of funds
   D. Cope with disruptions in routine
   E. Cope with sudden changes in the weather

DOMAIN V: Vocational

I. *The learner will obtain work*
   A. Seek employment
   B. Accept employment
   C. Use employment services

II. *The learner will perform the work routine*
   A. Perform the job routine
   B. Follow work-related daily schedule
   C. Maintain work station
   D. Follow employer rules and regulations
   E. Use facilities appropriately
   F. Follow job safety procedures
   G. Follow accident and emergency procedures

III. *The learner will coexist with others on the job*
   A. Interact appropriately with others on the job
   B. Cope with inappropriate conduct of others on the job

IV. *The learner will handle glitches on the job*
   A. Cope with changes in work routine
   B. Cope with work problems
   C. Cope with supply depletions and equipment breakdowns

DOMAIN L: Leisure

I. *The learner will develop leisure activities*
   A. Find new leisure activities
   B. Acquire skills for leisure activities

II. *The learner will follow leisure activity routines*
   A. Perform leisure activities
   B. Maintain leisure equipment
   C. Follow leisure safety procedures
   D. Follow accident and emergency procedures

III. *The learner will coexist with others during leisure*
   A. Interact appropriately with others in a leisure setting
   B. Respond to the inappropriate conduct of others

IV. *The learner will handle glitches during leisure*
   A. Cope with changes in leisure routine
   B. Cope with equipment breakdowns and material depletions

DOMAIN T: Travel

I. *The learner will travel routes in the community*
   A. Form mental maps of frequented buildings
   B. Form mental maps of the community

II. *The learner will use conveyances*
   A. Follow usage procedures
   B. Make decisions preparatory to travel
   C. Follow travel safety procedures
   D. Follow accident and emergency procedures

III. *The learner will coexist with others while traveling*
   A. Interact appropriately with others while traveling
   B. Respond to the inappropriate conduct of others while traveling

IV. *The learner will handle glitches during travel*
   A. Cope with changes in travel schedule
   B. Cope with equipment breakdowns
   C. Cope with being lost

DEVELOPMENT PROCEDURE

The basic procedure under which the taxonomy was developed was worked out during the conduct of another curriculum project (Dever, 1983). This procedure, which follows, was maintained during the entire taxonomy project.

Routines

The initial conceptual groundwork was laid by researchers at the University of Vermont, who developed a set of daily living routines for community residential facilities (Vogelsburg et al., 1980). The basic idea underlying them is that human beings are creatures of routine: most people do about the same thing every day. That is, we get out of bed at about the same time; we do the same things every morning before we go to work, we eat the same things consistently ("It must be Saturday because it's pizza"); and we even start bathing by touching the soap to our bodies in the same spot each time. Our daily life routines tend not to vary much, and even people who seem to have varied lives may not: rather they often just have routines that are different from those of most other persons.

This idea allowed a hypothesis to be formed. It should be possible to write out a set of basic routines that would characterize the life of most persons in the United States. Then, if independent persons (see Chapter 2) are those who go where others go, and do what the others do there, the routines would represent what people must do to be independent and would provide a statement of what learners should be taught.[6]

Therefore, the first group in the project developed a set of routines that seems to encapsulate the ordinary, day-to-day lives of most people (see Table 3-2). All groups that have participated in the project since that

---

[6] Note that some persons may never learn to generate *new* routines for themselves. In fact, they may have to perform the routines they have been taught automatically, with no adjustments for circumstances. Such automatism would put them in a position of "passing for normal" because they would lack the spontaneity required to adjust to changes in circumstances. Many workers will react negatively to this suggestion on the grounds that instruction that leads to this type of performance removes freedom of choice from the life of the individual. Certainly, those who teach will have to face up to this question at some time or other. Four facts are important in deciding whether or not to begin instruction that may lead to this state:

1. Humans naturally find routines comforting.

2. There can be no choice until a person has more than one thing from which to choose; further, learning to do two things requires a person to learn to do the first thing. Therefore, it is important to teach the first step, perhaps just in the hope that it will someday be possible to go on to the next step.

3. Those of us who are already independent may actually have very few choices to make. Not only are our choices limited by our responsibilities to others (family, friends, etc.), but also our behavior is limited by the setting in which we find ourselves (Barker, 1968) and by cultural rules governing such matters as speaking distances, touching, eye contact, verbal interactions, etc. Although these rules tend to be unwritten, those who break them are the recipients of very negative attention from others in the environment. Because our behavior is so closely governed by forces beyond our control, choices in any libertarian sense are sharply limited.

4. Many persons who are not taught to perform routines such as those presented in Table 3-1 will be reduced to having other people supervise them all the time. It is necessary to consider which is the lesser of two evils in such cases: that is, whether to teach automatisms or to foster dependence.

TABLE 3-2

Routines

a. Weekday Routine (Monday-Friday, Except Holidays)

1. Rise
2. Toilet
3. Groom self
4. Check weather conditions and select workday clothing
5. Dress
6. Make bed
7. Prepare breakfast
8. Eat breakfast
9. Prepare sack lunch
10. Clear table and wash dishes
11. Tidy kitchen
12. Brush teeth
13. Select outerwear for weather conditions
14. Check lights and appliances
15. Leave and secure house
16. Travel to work
    •
    •
    •
    (Perform work routine)
    •
    •
    •
17. Travel home (see also payday routine)
18. Collect mail
19. Store outerwear
20. Exercise
21. Select evening clothing (for chore/leisure routine)
22. Bathe
23. Groom and dress
24. Store dirty clothing (and linen, if applicable)
25. Tidy bathroom
26. Set table
27. Prepare supper
28. Eat
29. Clear table and wash dishes
30. Tidy kitchen
31. Tidy living room
32. Perform chore/leisure routine
33. Toilet and dress for bed
34. Set alarm
35. Sleep

TABLE 3-2 *(Continued)*

Routines

---

b. Payday Routine (see daily routine)

17a. Obtain paycheck
17b. Leave workplace
17c. Travel to bank
17d. Cash check, perform banking tasks
17e. Travel home
   •
   •
   •
   (same as #18-30 on daily routine)
   •
   •
   •

30a. Make food shopping list
30b. Check weather and select outer clothing
30c. Leave and secure house
30d. Travel to food store
30e. Shop for food
30f. Gather purchases and travel home
30g. Store purchases
   •
   •
   •
   (Same as #32-35 on daily routine)
   •
   •
   •

c. Saturday Routine

-
-
-

(#1-12 same as daily routine, except select Saturday chore clothing)

-
-
-

13. Select morning chores (see chore/leisure routine)
14. Check weather conditions and select outerwear according to chore
    (if outdoor chores required)
15. Do morning chores
16. Prepare lunch
17. Eat
18. Clear table and wash dishes
19. Tidy kitchen
20. Select Saturday leisure activity (see chore/leisure routine)
21. Select Saturday leisure clothing
22. Bathe and dress
23. Select outerwear according to weather conditions and activity
24. Perform leisure activity (see daily activities #14-16 if travel is involved)
25. Return home (if "away")

-
-
-

(same as #26-30 on daily routine, unless going to restaurant)

-
-
-

26. Select Saturday evening leisure clothing (change if necessary)
27. Select leisure activity
28. Check outerwear according to weather conditions (if "away")
29. Leave and secure house
30. Travel to leisure activity
31. Perform leisure activity
32. Return home

-
-
-

(same as #33-35 on daily routine)

-
-
-

TABLE 3-2   *(Continued)*

Routines

---

d. Sunday Routine

-
-
-

(#1-12 same as daily routine, except select Sunday clothing)

-
-
-

13. Select Sunday outerwear according to weather conditions
14. Check lights and appliances
15. Check appearance
16. Leave and secure house
17. Travel to church
18. Participate in service
19. Leave church
20. Travel home
21. Select leisure clothing
22. Change clothing (if necessary)
23. Perform leisure activity

-
-
-

(same as #16-29 on Saturday routine, except select Sunday leisure activities)

-
-
-

(same as #33-35 on daily routine)

e. Non-Daily Routine

Weekly Chore/Leisure Routine

Sunday:	morning	Church
		Sunday papers
	afternoon	Leisure activity (with friend(s))
	evening	Television, records
Monday:		Dampwipe appliances
		Wash wastebaskets
		Home leisure activity (alone or with friend(s))
Tuesday:		Set out garbage/trash for removal
		Sweep and mop bathroom and kitchen
		Home leisure activity (alone or with friend(s))
Wednesday:		Change beds
		Do laundry
		Home leisure activity (alone or with friend(s))
Thursday:		Inventory foodstock
		Clean refrigerator
		Home or away leisure activity (alone or with friend(s))
Friday:		Shop for food
		Pay bills
		Home leisure activity (alone or with friend(s))
Saturday:	morning	Dust and vacuum living quarters
		Shake rugs
		Change bath linens
		Clean sinks, mirrors, commode, cupboards
		Tidy rooms
		Perform monthly/seasonal chores
	afternoon	Perform home or away leisure activity with friend(s)
	evening	Perform away leisure activity with friend(s)

Monthly Chore Routine	Sort magazines
	Wash fixtures
	Wash floors
	Clean furniture
	Tidy closets
	Pay bills
Monthly Leisure Routine	Visit with family
Seasonal Chore Routine	Wash blankets
	Defrost refrigerator
	Change screens/storm windows
	Clean under large appliances
	Turn mattress
	Wash windows
	Cut grass/shovel snow
	Lubricate mechanicals
	Store equipment
Seasonal Leisure Activities	Attend events (basketball, football, baseball, etc.)
	Participate in sports (swimming, skiing, etc.)
	Attend classes

TABLE 3-2   *(Continued)*

Routines

Annual Chores	Clean gutters
	Paint
	Wash outdoor furniture
	Clean basement/storage
	Prune trees/bushes
	Plant
	Clean furniture/airconditioner
	Clean closets
Annual Leisure Activities	Holiday celebrations
	Vacations
Occasional Chores	Replace fuses/bulbs
	Replace broken/worn equipment
	Replace broken/worn house parts
	Clean up after accidents
	Replace toilet paper, soap, etc.
	Mend clothing/shoes

have agreed that these routines fairly represent the manner in which most of us go through our daily lives. For example, each of us gets up, attends to our daily ablutions, eats, secures our living quarters, and goes to work. When we get to the job we go through a settling-in subroutine, perform our jobs, take breaks, etc., and stop work at some point. The routines for individuals seem to vary only in details; for example, some people work on the second or third shift, some people do not eat breakfast or make the bed, and some people get cleaned up when they come home from work instead of before they go. But such details are not important to the notion inherent in the routines themselves.

Skills

If persons who are not independent learn to perform routines similar to those in Table 3-1, their need for supervision will be reduced and they will become more independent. Further, if they learn a sufficient number of routines, their need for supervision will be reduced to zero. At that point, they will in fact be independent.

Therefore, the next step was to analyze the routines to find out what skills are required to perform them without extraordinary assistance. This step resulted in the lists of goals that appear in the taxonomy. The analysis was carried out in the following manner.

Each step in the routines was analyzed to discover how many things we might have to do to perform the routines. This step resulted in the list of the major goals. For example, to maintain employment workers must get along with the bosses and fellow employees. Because people who do not get along with their bosses and fellow employees risk losing their employment, learning to get along with the boss and fellow employees is a skill that people must learn in order to become independent. Therefore, it became a goal in the Vocational Domain.

Next, each goal was analyzed in an attempt to derive a list of skills required to accomplish each of the items identified in the previous step. Thus, to buy clothes, a person must be able to go to the store; select a purchase; pay for the purchase; leave the store with the purchase. A person who develops a way to do these things will attain the outcome of purchasing clothing no matter what method he must use to do so (White, 1980). This analysis yielded the lists of subgoals that appear under each major goal.

A number of lists were developed, discussed, added to, deleted from, and eventually organized into the domains. Overlaps were resolved, duplications were eliminated, and the lists were put into final form. The lists of goals and their subgoals constitute the taxonomy. Again, no attempt has been made to analyze further for the purpose of developing either curricula or programs. Both of these tasks are most properly carried out by agencies in individual communities.

Numbering System

The taxonomy is indexed. Its numbering system follows an outline arranged as follows:

Domains are indicated with a letter:

P	Personal Maintenance and Development
H	Homemaking and Community Life
V	Vocational
L	Leisure
T	Travel

Subdomains are indicated by Roman numerals. There are four in each domain. For example:

V/I	Goals Related to Finding a Job
H/II	Goals Related to Community Life Routines
P/III	Goals Related to Establishing and Maintaining Personal Relationships
T/IV	Goals Related to Handling Glitches While Traveling

Goals are indicated by a capital letter. For example:

P/II A   The Learner Will Use Appropriate First Aid and Illness Treatment Procedures

H/IV D   The Learner Will Respond Appropriately to Sudden Changes in the Weather

Skills are indicated by a decimal system that can extend indefinitely to indicate successive subclassifications, such as:

2.01

4.06.03

5.04.11.03

The latter have varying degrees of specificity, according to the need each goal presents.

CONCLUDING STATEMENT

A taxonomy is only an organization of something. As is true for definitions, organizations are neither correct nor incorrect; rather, they can only be useful or not useful. This taxonomy classifies daily life in the community in an attempt to make it useful for the purpose of assisting curriculum construction.

The domains were selected to allow daily life in the community to be classified with ease. The outline allows easy computerization and the skills listed provide a template of the community and of the things people must do to live within it unsupervised.

As part of the development project, a national survey was conducted to obtain the reactions of professionals in the field. Although many expressed objections to parts of the taxonomy or its presentation (which objections have been responded to in this final document), the response was generally favorable (Dever, 1987). The probable reason for the good reception is that the taxonomy meets a deeply felt need for clear instructional goals. In meeting this need, this manual makes a unique contribution to the field.

There is yet much to do, however. For example, the curricula for teaching persons to live in the community unsupervised have yet to be constructed and techniques for using those curricula to derive individual programs of instruction have yet to be developed. Therefore, in a very real sense, this taxonomy represents only the opening move in what promises to be a very long and complicated procedure.

Chapter 4

Constructing An Agency Curriculum
by Dennis R. Knapczyk

INTRODUCTION

Focus of Chapter

This chapter provides guidelines that agency personnel can use to construct a curriculum to suit the unique needs of the agency, the learners served by the agency, and the community in which the agency is located. The curriculum that results from following these guidelines is one that can facilitate both the development of quality instructional programs for individual learners and the planning of consistent and continuous instructional services across administrative units within the agency. Specifically, the chapter will describe the steps that an agency, rather than an individual instructor, should complete to construct a curriculum to organize its instructional programs.

In this chapter the term *curriculum* refers to a document composed of organized sets of objectives that progress sequentially toward a predetermined goal or series of endpoints. The goal and endpoints of the curriculum provide a frame of reference for determining which objectives are contained in the curriculum (Gay, 1980). The listing of curriculum objectives indicates the range and progression of skills a learner must display to achieve the goal and represents milestones of educational progress (Tuckman & Edwards, 1971).

It must be noted that the term *curriculum*, when applied to the instruction of learners who are low functioning, can refer to products containing elements other than curriculum objectives. For example, some authors (e.g., Gaylord-Ross & Holvoet, 1985; Sailor & Guess, 1983; Snell, 1987; Wilcox & Bellamy, 1982) indicate that a curriculum should also include such elements as task analyses, functional analyses of target responses, and descriptions of instructional activities, methodologies, and materials.

These authors state (or imply) that the responsibility for constructing a curriculum rests with individual instructors and, consequently, the authors tend to include all or most of the steps in the instructional paradigm within the curriculum development process.

In this chapter, constructing a curriculum is viewed as the responsibility of the community agency, e.g., rehabilitation center, school system, or residential center, and should result from the cooperative efforts of the entire staff. When a curriculum is the product of an agency rather than an individual instructor, it is likely that the instructional services that result from its use will receive greater support from agency personnel and the community as a whole. In addition, an agency curriculum can (a) serve as a referent for establishing priorities for staff and resource allocation; (b) provide a focal point for structuring staff development and planning activities; and (c) provide a standard against which to monitor and evaluate agency programs. As indicated in Chapter 2, when the staff of an agency constructs a curriculum, it must clearly distinguish between the curricular and programming aspects of the instructional paradigm.

Information Needed to Construct an Agency Curriculum

Agencies that provide instructional services to persons who are low functioning should use curricula with sequenced sets of objectives that progress toward independence in community settings (Guess et al., 1978; Rusch & Mithaug, 1985; Wacker & Hoffman, 1984). The curricula will vary from agency to agency because there are a multitude of settings in which performance can occur and a wide variety of ways in which people can demonstrate independence in any of these settings. Therefore, to produce a curriculum that can guide quality instructional programs, it is necessary to limit the contents of a curriculum to those options most applicable to the persons who will be taught using the curriculum. For example, there are many different ways through which a person can become gainfully employed but only a small sample of the alternatives will be available to any one learner. Similarly, although there is a wide array of settings in which persons can participate in recreational and entertainment activities, individual learners will have the proficiency or interest to participate in only a small sample of these settings. Those engaged in curriculum development must first determine which subsets of options apply to the learners served by the agency and then use the subsets to develop the objectives contained in the curriculum. The taxonomy can serve as an important resource in determining which options pertain to the learners because it provides an organizational structure for (a) deciding which areas of independence apply to the learners; (b) establishing instructional endpoints to suit their needs; and (c) identifying the community settings in which they will exhibit goal-related performance.

Constructing a curriculum also requires that the agency attend to three sources of information: the characteristics of the learners participating in the agency's programs; the characteristics of the settings in which learners will ultimately perform skills; and the characteristics of the agency itself. As illustrated in Figure 4-1, each source of information contributes unique elements to the process of constructing a curriculum and adds further refinement to the curriculum objectives and pathways. Close attention to the sources of information will facilitate the planning and organization of the curriculum; enhance the clarity of its content; and increase its usefulness in planning instructional programs and activities. For example, the mission of an agency and the resources available for instruction will affect which subset of goals will serve as endpoints for the curriculum pathways. The characteristics of the learners will determine the number and types of lead-up and prerequisite skills that are contained in the pathways. Finally, the characteristics of the settings in which performance will ultimately occur will dictate the conditions of performance and the standards for the curriculum objectives that comprise the pathways.

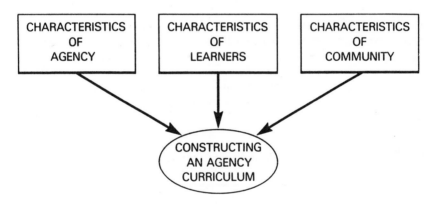

FIGURE 4-1: Sources of Information Needed to Construct A Curriculum for Persons Who Are Low-Functioning.

Constructing a curriculum also requires coordination among the various agencies within a community that are responsible for providing instruction to persons who are low functioning. For example, the sequence of objectives contained in the curriculum of one agency will probably overlap those of other agencies because it is necessary to ensure that all potential endpoints and outcomes pertaining to community functioning can be addressed by at least one of the agencies. Therefore, even though each curriculum will contain a different series of curriculum objectives, the agencies in a community should take steps to ensure that:

1. The sum total of all the curriculum objectives contained in agency curricula will allow any individual learner in the community service network to progress toward independence in an orderly and systematic manner; and

2. Any overlap of curriculum objectives or duplication of instructional services will be closely coordinated across agencies and monitored by them to achieve consistency in programming.

To avoid the fragmentation and duplication of instructional services that often characterize community service networks, the missions, roles, and responsibilities for instructional services provided by agencies within a community must complement one another (Halpern, 1985; Will; 1984; Zais, 1976). The process of constructing a curriculum can be an effective vehicle for achieving cooperation in the area of instructional services.

STEPS TO CONSTRUCTING AN AGENCY CURRICULUM

The steps required to construct a curriculum for use in a community agency are outlined in Figure 4-2. Completing each step requires close attention to the different sections of the taxonomy as well as the characteris-

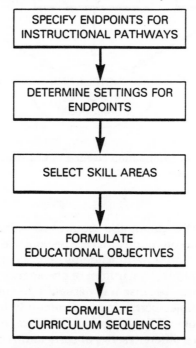

FIGURE 4-2: Steps to Constructing An Agency Curriculum.

tics of the community, the agency, and the persons served by the agency. In this section each of the steps will be examined in detail.

Specify Endpoints for Instructional Pathways

The first step in devising an agency curriculum is to examine the goals in each domain and select those endpoints that best represent the focus of the agency's instructional programs. Some agencies will attend to endpoints from only one of the domains, while other agencies will choose endpoints from more than one (and possibly all) of the domains. The characteristics of the agency will provide the basis for selecting endpoints.

In any community, each agency will probably choose a different composite of endpoints around which to formulate its curriculum. For example, a community agency may specifically develop instructional programs in the Homemaking and Community Life Domain because its mission is to establish alternative independent living options in the community. The endpoints of the curriculum for this agency may include such items from the taxonomy as

Keeping Living Quarters Neat and Clean (H/II A)
Keeping Fabric Items Clean and Repaired (H/II B)
Preparing and Serving Meals (H/II I)

and others pertinent to maintaining a homelike environment. In contrast, another agency, whose mission is to prepare persons for job placement in competitive work settings, may assume responsibility for such items in the Vocational Domain as

Performing a Job Routine (V/II A)
Following Work-Related Daily Schedules (V/II B)
Maintaining a Work Station (V/II C)

and similar items. Some agencies, like the public schools, will take responsibility for providing instructional services across all of the domains and will select endpoints for their curricula accordingly.

Learner Considerations

Those who construct curricula for young adults and children will find that many of the endpoints listed in the taxonomy are not age appropriate for those learners. For example, even many students in general education do not learn how to obtain their own apartments, budget money effectively, or assess job desirability before they graduate from the public schools. Although these endpoints may not be appropriate for low-functioning learners in public school special education programs, adopting them as endpoints for the curriculum ensures that the prerequisite and lead-up skills associated with them will not be overlooked.

Establishing Program Priorities

Early in the process of constructing a curriculum, it is important for agency personnel to begin establishing priorities among the instructional endpoints selected for the curriculum. A review of the instructional endpoints selected for the curriculum will show that some are more important to achieving independence in the community than others are. For example, some endpoints are essential to participating in community settings and will apply to most learners in an agency's programs. Some examples:

Maintaining Personal Cleanliness (P/I A)
Grooming Self (P/I B)
Interacting Appropriately with Others in the Community (H/III A)
Performing Leisure Activities (L/II A)

Other endpoints will be important because their performance will permit at least partial participation in community activities or will increase the quality of life of the learners. For example, Maintaining Good Nutritional Habits (P/I E) and Exercising Regularly (P/I F) are important instructional endpoints because performance in these areas can help increase learners' stamina, alertness, and overall ability to participate in instructional and community activities (Ford et al., 1984; Patton, Payne, & Bierne-Smith, 1986). Other endpoints, such as Preparing and Serving Meals (H/II I) and Performing a Job Routine (V/II A), are important because they reduce learners' dependence on others for direction and supervision, or because they improve the social status of the learners in the community (Rusch, Chadsey-Rusch, & Lagomarcino, 1987).

Some endpoints can be placed lower on the list of priorities because provisions can be made to postpone or circumvent the need for the skills in the learners' particular circumstances. For example, instruction in some areas of homemaking can be postponed until after the learners can perform the basic homemaking routines. The following are examples of endpoints that may be postponed under certain circumstances.

Maintaining the Exterior of the Living Quarters (H/II D)
Budgeting Money (H/II J)
Paying Bills (H/II K)
Following Emergency Procedures (H/II G)

Similarly, the procedures used by an agency to match persons to specific work settings may reduce the need for instruction in such areas as Responding Appropriately to the Inappropriate Conduct of Others on the Job (V/III B) or Coping With Changes in the Work Routine or Schedule (V/IV A and V/IV B). Finally, other endpoints, such as Finding Appropriate Living Quarters (H/I A) and Seeking Employment (V/I A), may be of even lower priority if community services are available to provide assistance to the learners.

Falvey (1986) listed several factors related to the characteristics of the learners and their community that are useful in setting priorities for instructional programs. For example, Falvey stated that curriculum endpoints should represent skills that:

1. Are required across environments;

2. Are used frequently by the person;

3. Conform to family and community demands;

4. Are comparable to performance required of peers;

5. Lead to increased participation in community settings; and

6. Promote overall independence.

Setting priorities for the curriculum endpoints requires input and cooperation from a wide variety of community members, including parents, neighbors, local merchants, civic leaders, community service personnel, and others (Ford et al., 1984; Wehman, Kregel, & Barcus, 1985). For example, it is essential to consult a representative sample of potential employers of the learners before deciding which goals within the Vocational Domain must be emphasized within the agency curriculum.

Specify the Settings for Curriculum Endpoints

After the endpoints for the curriculum have been established, the next step in constructing a curriculum involves identifying those settings that correspond most closely to the circumstances under which the learners will ultimately display performance. The referents for a curriculum must include both the settings that constitute current environments and potential future environments in which learners will display performance (Brown, Branston, Hamre-Nietupski, Pumpian, Certo, & Gruenewald, 1979; Snell, 1987).

In any community there are a variety of different settings in which persons must ultimately display the skills represented by the endpoints. For example, Performing Leisure Activities (L/II A) can occur in a neighborhood park, an arcade in a shopping mall, a fast food restaurant, in the person's home or backyard, or in any number of other settings. Similarly, Performing a Job Routine (V/II A) can take place in a local manufacturing industry, a motel, a small business, or many other employment locations. Each alternative location constitutes a setting for performance and each will create opportunities for producing outcomes based upon the situational variables and standards that characterize the setting (Rusch & Mithaug, 1985).

Limit the Range of Settings

For purposes of constructing a curriculum, the range of possible settings must be limited to those that best represent the types of settings in which persons will ultimately perform the skills represented by the endpoints. By limiting the number of settings that serve as referents for the curriculum, instruction can focus upon those settings in which learners have the greatest potential for participation (Ford et al., 1984). For example, the range of possible settings in which learners can gain employment or participate in leisure activities will be limited by the learners' interest, aptitude, or opportunities to participate in them (Moon, Goodall, Barcus, & Brooke, 1985). Clearly, the usefulness of the agency's curriculum will be determined by the degree to which the curriculum objectives reflect the settings in which persons will most likely participate (Snell, 1987). Falvey (1986), Ford et al. (1984), Wilcox and Bellamy (1982), and others have identified several factors to consider in selecting community settings to serve as referents for the curriculum objectives. They indicate that these settings should:

1. Be age appropriate to the learners in the program;

2. Provide variety for the learners;

3. Be proximate to the primary settings in which the learners live and work;

4. Be preferred by the learners (i.e., consistent with their interests, aptitudes, and physical characteristics);

5. Be consistent with the lifestyles of the learners' families, friends, and acquaintances;

6. Allow adaptations or permit alternative forms of performance suitable to the characteristics of the learners;

7. Provide opportunities for skill development across functional areas of performance; and

8. Be suitable for in-situ training.

Settings As Referents for the Agency Curriculum

For some endpoints in the curriculum, a sampling of community settings will be needed as referents; for other endpoints, only one or two settings will be required. For example, in the Leisure Domain, a range of settings should serve as the referents for such endpoints as:

Performing Leisure Activities (L/II A)
Following Leisure Safety Procedures (L/II C)
Interacting Appropriately with Others During Leisure Activities
   (L/III A)

Leisure settings will place very different demands on persons depending on such characteristics as activity (e.g., team sports, crafts); location (e.g., within the home, outside in the neighborhood, in the community); type of participation (e.g., spectator or participant); cost (e.g., free or requiring an admission charge); need for other participants (e.g., performed individually, in small groups, or as part of the crowd); and use of supplies and equipment (e.g., sports equipment, safety gear). Agencies should select an array of settings across dimensions such as these in order to assist in developing a comprehensive set of curriculum objectives that suit the characteristics of the learners, provide for variety, and maintain consistency with family and personal preferences and lifestyles (Ford et al., 1984). Similarly, to ensure that learners are adequately prepared for the different work opportunities available to them in the community, it will often be necessary to select several different work settings as referents for such endpoints as:

Performing the Job Routine (V/II A)
Following Work-Related Schedules (V/II B)
Maintaining a Work Station (V/II C)

For some endpoints community surveys can provide very useful information in selecting referents from the array of settings available. Examples might be surveys of leisure activities conducted on family and friends (Falvey, 1986; Ford et al., 1984) and those conducted to assess the availability of work settings (Easterday & Sitlington, 1985; Moon et al., 1985).

For other endpoints it would be necessary to specify only one or two locations that best represent the possible options the learners may encounter. Thus, it may be sufficient to use only one or two banks, churches, or fast food restaurants as referents for devising curriculum objectives. Similarly, it is often best to use the learner's current living arrangements as the basis for specifying curriculum objectives in the Homemaking and Community Life Domain, especially for endpoints such as:

Maintaining Personal Cleanliness (P/I A)
Keeping Living Quarters Neat and Clean (H/II A)
Maintaining a Foodstock (H/II H)

Table 4-1 provides examples of referent settings for selected endpoints in the taxonomy.

TABLE 4-1

Examples of Settings That Can Be Used as Referents for Endpoints

Endpoint: Travel to Locations within Community (T/I A4)
Referent Settings: Sam's Barber Shop
                             First National Bank
                             Crosstown Food Mart
                             St. Mark's Church
                             Main Street Cinema

Endpoint: Keep Fabric Items Clean and Repaired (H/II B)
Referent Settings: Laundry room in apartment complex
                             Sunshine Cleaners on North Main Street

Endpoint: Maintain Personal Cleanliness (P/I A)
Referent Settings: McDonald's Restaurant on East Fifth Street
                             Walter's Department Store
                             Central Park
                             East Side YMCA
                             Learner's home

Instruction provided in the environment in which learners will ultimately display performance represented by the endpoints will enhance rapid acquisition of skills and reduce the need for teaching generalization of the skills learned in noninstructional settings (Snell, 1987). Consequently, curriculum objectives that focus instruction in this manner make it possible to increase the continuity and consistency of instruction as learners progress through the agency's programs. Any subsequent generalization training needed to assist learners to adapt to different settings can then be handled individually as needed (Horner, Sprague, & Wilcox, 1982).

Limit the Range of Settings

In selecting settings that will be used as referents for the agency curriculum, it is important to consider changes in the community or the learners' lifestyles that may affect the number and range of settings to which they will have access following instruction. For example, instructional settings available to an agency can be affected by state or regional plans to establish a supported employment or independent living program, the addition or deletion of a community service, or the opening or closing of a local industry. To provide another example: it may be possible that a home setting other than that in which the learners currently live may be the most appropriate referent in programs for adolescents and young adults. Such a setting would permit formulation of curriculum objectives that can facilitate the transition to living outside a family unit.

Select Skill Areas That Pertain to Instructional Endpoints and Settings

Figure 4-2 shows that the next step in constructing a curriculum is to determine which of the skill areas listed as subheadings in the taxonomy apply to the instructional endpoints and settings selected for the curriculum. The items in the taxonomy illustrate the areas of performance that pertain to reaching an endpoint in the settings in which performance occurs.

Expectations of Settings

The skill areas selected from the taxonomy should correspond to the performance demands learners must meet to achieve independence in the settings used as referents for the curriculum (Bronfenbrenner, 1977; Rusch & Mithaug, 1985). For example, in the domestic settings selected as referents for the curriculum, Maintaining the Exterior of the Living Quarters (H/II D) may require the learners to:

Keep Debris from Accumulating (H/II D1)
Wash Exterior Windows and Storm Fixtures (H/II D2)
Keep Walks Clear of Ice and Snow (H/II D7)

The other skill areas listed under the endpoint may not be required because of the circumstances that pertain to the setting. For example, learners may live in an apartment, have no outdoor furniture, and have a lawn care service cut the grass and trim the shrubs. If so, their situation would negate the need to consider the other skill areas for this endpoint. Similarly, in the vocational settings selected for the curriculum, Following Safety Procedures While on the Job (V/II F) may require learners to:

Use and Store Tools and Materials Appropriately (V/II F1 and F2)
Keep the Job Station Neat and Free of Safety Hazards (V/II F4)
Follow Supervisor's Directions in Unusual Circumstances (V/II F7)

The other skill areas listed for this endpoint may not apply to the settings available for employment. Thus, close inspection of the lists of skill areas under the endpoints in the taxonomy will assist in determining the types of performance persons must exhibit to achieve independence in the community settings selected for the curriculum. Table 4-2 shows examples of skill areas that may apply to a setting serving as a referent for a curriculum endpoint.

TABLE 4-2

Examples of Skill Areas That Can Apply to Community Settings

Endpoints: Budget Money Appropriately (H/II J) and Pay Bills (H/II K)

Referent Settings:	City National Bank
Skill Areas:	Cash Checks (H/II J2)
	Maintain Savings Account (H/II J3.01)
	Maintain Checking Account (H/II J3.02)
	Pay Utility Bills (H/II K1.03)
	Deposit Savings (H/II K3)

Endpoints: Find Appropriate Leisure Activities (L/I A) and Acquire Skills Required (L/I B): Attend a Movie at a Cinema

Referent Settings:	Central Mall Cinema
Skill Areas:	Use Advertisements to Identify Leisure Activity (L/I A1.01.01)
	Use Friends to Identify Leisure Activity (L/I A1.02.02)
	Assess Entertainment Value of Activity (L/I A2.01.03)
	Assess Social Benefits of Activity (L/I A2.01.01)
	Assess Accessibility of Activity (L/I A2.03)
	Assess Ability to Pay Admission (L/I A3.01.01)
	Acquire Skills Informally Through Friends (L/I B2.02.01)
	Acquire Skills Informally through Participants (L/I B2.02.02)

Determining Skill Areas for Curriculum

By considering the characteristics of the referent community settings and the agency, those constructing a curriculum can limit the number of skill areas to those that are most pertinent to learners.

Considerations That Pertain to the Community Settings. Information about the characteristics of the community in which the learners live is important in selecting the skill areas contained within the curriculum (Schultz, Williams, Iverson, & Duncan, 1984). For example, an agency that provides instruction in the Travel Domain must consider the alternate forms of public and private transportation available in the community. Examination of these options will determine which areas will need to be addressed in the curriculum objectives. Endpoints for which this determination is necessary include the following:

Following Usage Procedures for Conveyances (T/II A)
Making Decisions Preparatory to Travel (T/II B)
Following Safety Procedures (T/II C)
Interacting Appropriately with Others While Traveling (T/III A)

In communities where learners have access to a public transportation system, skill areas pertaining to its use will be an important part of the agency curriculum. However, in many rural and suburban areas without public transportation, items relating to pedestrian travel and the use of agency or private transportation will be more pertinent to the agency's curriculum. Similarly, agencies responsible for providing instruction in the Vocational Domain will find that some of the items listed pertain to employment in manufacturing or industrial settings, while others relate to employment in service or small business settings. Accordingly, those engaged in devising a curriculum must select skill areas for such endpoints as:

Following Employer's Rules and Regulations (V/II D)
Using Employer Facilities (V/II E)
Following Safety Procedures (V/II F)

Comparable differences will be found for items in the Homemaking and Community Life Domain for agencies preparing persons to live in apartment dwellings, duplexes, or houses.

Considerations That Pertain to the Agency. The characteristics of the agency also will affect the selection of skill areas contained within the curriculum. The following features of an agency will have to be considered:

1. *Facility and Resources.* The facility and the resources available for instruction can affect the types of skills that will be the focus of instruction. An agency providing instruction in the Homemaking and Community Life Domain will find that many of the items listed in the taxonomy require physical resources, such as access to both home or apartment-like facilities and to the supplies and equipment typically contained in them. For example, instruction in skills for Keeping Living Quarters Neat and Clean (H/II A) requires that facilities and supplies be available for vacuuming, dusting furniture, and washing and cleaning a variety of surfaces. Similarly, instruction in the area of Keeping Fabric Items Clean and Repaired (H/II B) requires access to many different types of fabric items and the equipment to wash, dry, and store them. Finally, instruction in skills for Maintaining the Exterior of Living Quarters (H/II D) requires a homelike environment that needs regular maintenance.

If the agency does not have access to the physical resources to complement these areas, it will not be possible to develop effective instructional programs to teach the skills. It must be noted, however, that community-based instructional programs can reduce an agency's need for owning space or purchasing the resources to support instruction in many areas. For example, it may not be necessary to purchase cleaning supplies and equipment if an agency arranges to use those already available in the learner's home or at a nearby hotel or motel. Therefore, for those constructing a curriculum, discovering ways to gain access to resources and facilities is sometimes more important than building an inventory of agency resources and facilities.

2. *Policies and Procedures.* The policies and procedures established by the agency can also limit the types of skill areas to be included in the curriculum. The items selected must take into account policies regarding such issues as the sexual conduct of the learners, the exposure of learners to potentially dangerous situations, and the supervision of learners in community settings. For example, some of the skills in the Vocational Domain require an agency to structure opportunities for learners to respond to equipment breakdowns, work stoppages, harassment by fellow workers, and on-the-job emergencies. Some examples of endpoints with such requirements include:

Following Accident and Emergency Procedures (V/II G)
Coping With Work Problems (V/IV B)
Responding to Inappropriate Conduct of Others While
    on the Job (V/III B)

For example, as part of most manufacturing jobs, workers must learn to handle equipment malfunctions or breakdowns, supply shortages, or defective materials. Even though learners will have to display such skills in competitive employment settings, an agency may be unwilling or unable to permit development of instructional activities suitable to train learners in these areas. Under such circumstances these skill areas cannot reasonably be part of the agency's curriculum.

3. *Staffing Patterns and Schedules.* The manner in which staff and instructional time blocks are scheduled is another factor that can affect selection of skill areas. For example, instructional time slots may be scheduled in small increments to allow for provision of ancillary or support services, or to permit employees to have breaks on a rotating basis. Such scheduling procedures can limit instruction in areas such as:

Preparing and Serving Meals (H/II I2 and H/II I3)
Following Daily Work Schedules (V/II B1)
Engaging in Leisure Activities (L/II A3)

That is, because of an agency's program schedule, there may be insufficient time for learners to perform the requisite skills or to integrate skills into complex routines. Similarly, the employment schedules of the staff may prevent instruction on many items. For example, some skills may require instruction during times when the agency is not typically in operation, such as evenings and weekends. Examples include:

Interacting Appropriately with Family and Friends
(P/III A and P/III B)
Traveling to and Interacting in Religious Services
(T/I B4 and L/III A)
Maintaining Appropriate Sleep Patterns (P/I D)
Responding to the Inappropriate Conduct of Others
in the Community (H/III B)

If it is not possible to schedule instructional activities during these times, skills in these areas cannot become an integral component of the agency's curriculum.

Changing An Agency to Expand Instructional Programming Options

In conjunction with selecting skill areas to include in a curriculum, it is important that the agency review the policies and procedures that govern its instructional programs and examine the use of current and future resources (Falvey, 1986). For example, as items are considered for inclusion in the curriculum, a determination can be made regarding the availability of resources or status of policies and procedures that pertain to providing instruction in that area. Accordingly, items can be placed into one of three categories: those for which the agency can provide instruction within the existing organization and structure of the programs; those that require a change in policy or procedures; and those that cannot be added to the curriculum until there is a change in the manner in which existing resources are allocated or until additional resources become available. As skills are placed into the second and third categories, the agency can develop a plan and a timeline through which resources can be generated and requisite policies and procedures developed. Then, decisions regarding improvements in the instructional programs can be made deliberately and systematically as part of the process of constructing a curriculum.

Formulating Curriculum Objectives for Curriculum Endpoints and Skills

Figure 4-2 shows that the next step in constructing an agency curriculum is to formulate curriculum objectives. This step requires specifying the conditions under which performance is to occur and setting the stan-

dards that govern performance under these conditions (Alberto & Troutman, 1986; Mager, 1962). For each skill area and each setting serving as
referents for the curriculum, there are conditions or sets of situational
variables in effect within the setting at the time of performance. Concomit-
antly, there are sets of standards that indicate the requirements a person's
performance must meet to achieve the desired outcome (Bailey, 1982). The
result of specifying the variables and standards that pertain to the circumstances under which learners will exhibit performance in community
settings will be curriculum objectives.

Specifying the Conditions of Performance

In most settings, there are a variety of different situations under which
performance can occur. The circumstances for performance can vary along
many dimensions, including the number and type of people present in the
setting, the materials and equipment available, the time of day, the type
of surroundings, and many other factors. For example, a person who orders
a meal at a fast food restaurant can do so at an inside counter or at an
outside display panel. He can place his order during a rush period or in a
lull time, and can make his selections when the breakfast or the dinner
menu is being prepared. In addition, he can choose to eat the meal at the
restaurant or carry out the items. Each of these alternatives constitutes a
different set of conditions under which performance can occur. Similarly,
a person can perform a job at the worksite when there is a rush to complete
the job or when there is not enough work for the employees to do, when
fellow workers and job supervisors create a supportive work atmosphere
or when they create one filled with tension and animosity, and when the
work routine is very regimented or when it is flexible and selected by the
worker. Comparable differences in the conditions of performance can arise
at home and in leisure and travel settings. Each set of conditions in a setting
places a different set of demands on a learner's performance (Bronfenbrenner, 1977). The learners' performance must correspond to the existing conditions in order for them to participate successfully in the setting and
produce the desired outcomes (Mook, 1987; Rusch & Mithaug, 1985). Therefore, because they determine the types of performance learners must display
in community settings, the conditions must be specified for each of the
skills selected for the curriculum and for the referent settings corresponding
to the skills.

In most instances, it will not be feasible or even possible to provide
instruction across the entire range of conditions that persons might encounter in a setting. Consequently, those engaged in constructing a curriculum must decide which conditions will become the focus of the agency's
instructional programs. The characteristics of the learners and the community settings in which they will function will be important sources of infor-

mation in determining the conditions for the skills selected for the agency curriculum.

For some skills, the range of situations learners will encounter in a setting will be limited by their preferences or by the preferences of their family and friends (Ford et al., 1984). For other skills, it may be possible for the agency to recommend that changes be made in the setting, that is, within a home or a place of employment.

It may also be advantageous to suggest that learners' participation should occur under some conditions but not others in order to increase the degree of participation or success they can have in a setting. For example, performance requirements associated with shopping vary considerably depending upon how crowded the shopping areas are and the number of items from which selections must be made. That is, shopping for groceries on Saturday morning or for clothing a week before Christmas places different demands on performance than does shopping during less crowded times. If arrangements can be made to have learners shop under a specified set of conditions (e.g., nonpeak times), a less stringent set of performance requirements can be incorporated into the curriculum objectives. Making these decisions early in the process of formulating curriculum objectives will assist agency personnel in devising home, work, or community performance routines to take advantage of the changing conditions occurring within and across settings and to maximize the learners' participation in the community (Moon et al., 1985). Such arrangements should be made in conjunction with specifying the conditions for the curriculum objectives contained in the curriculum.

When it is probable that learners will participate under a range of conditions in a setting, it may be necessary to select a representative sample of situations to serve as referents for performance (Horner, McDonnell, & Bellamy, 1986; Horner, Sprague, & Wilcox, 1982). For example, when using a public transportation system, it is likely that learners must learn to perform in a variety of different circumstances, such as paying the fare when they have correct change and when they do not; riding the vehicle when there are many seats available, a few seats available, or no seats available; and boarding or leaving the vehicle when they are the only ones present and when they must form a queue with other riders. In instances such as these, two or more situations may be required as referents for specifying the conditions of performance to ensure that the curriculum objectives accurately reflect requirements for successful participation in the setting.

In some settings in which conditions are changeable from performance to performance, assistance may be naturally available in the environment to help persons adapt to the different circumstances that may arise. For example, clerks in clothing stores often offer assistance in locating items, checking for size and fit, and paying for purchases. Similarly, bus drivers on the routes that learners frequently travel may be willing to assist the public in boarding and leaving the bus, paying their fares, and locating their destinations. Under circumstances such as these, the conditions of performance need only reflect the essential requirements for performance.

Identifying Standards for Curriculum Objectives

Preparing curriculum objectives also involves specifying the standards that apply to the skills selected for the curriculum. Standards refer to the criteria or minimum level of performance required to produce the desired outcomes (Bailey, 1982). In most instances, different standards will apply to each of the skills, settings, and conditions serving as referents for the curriculum (Rusch & Mithaug, 1985). Those engaged in constructing a curriculum can determine which standards apply to performance by analyzing the outcomes and performance requirements that pertain to the conditions under which performance is to occur (Bailey, 1982; Snell & Browder, 1986).

Identify Outcomes of Performance.   Outcomes are any effects a person's actions have upon the environment. They provide useful indicators for judging when a person's performance is *acceptable* or *appropriate* because they can be seen, heard, tasted, etc. By establishing a benchmark for how the outcomes should appear to an observer, those devising a curriculum can establish an objective set of criteria and a measurement system for the performance of the learners in the instructional programs. Standards will apply to the outcomes for each of the skills specified within the agency curriculum. Thus, standards can be set for the taste of foods to be prepared, the number of products to be completed by the end of the workday, and the elapsed time between the start and finish of an activity.

Identify Performance Requirements.[7]   The performance requirements for the outcomes can provide an additional set of criteria for the curriculum objectives (Guess & Helmstetter, 1986). The types of actions required, along with the sequence and contiguity of these actions, can indicate the series of accomplishments that persons must complete to produce an outcome (Mook, 1987). These accomplishments, and the criteria that pertain to them, provide a means for dividing those curriculum objectives requiring complex performance routines into component objectives each of which can serve

---

[7] Identifying performance requirements should not be confused with listing steps in a task analysis. Performance requirements pertain to the series of accomplishments involved in producing an outcome and are established by the conditions that exist in a setting. In contrast, a task analysis lists the actions learners exhibit to produce the accomplishments. It is determined by each learner's individual learning and performance characteristics. Under a specific set of conditions, the performance requirements will remain constant. However, the manner in which learners meet the performance requirements as described in a task analysis can vary considerably from learner to learner (Mook, 1987; White, 1980).

as a milestone for instruction. In many instances these components can serve as lead-up objectives in the agency curriculum (Bailey, 1982).

Setting Standards for Curriculum Objectives

There are two steps involved in setting standards for the curriculum objectives. These steps are described in the next sections.

Specify Outcomes and Performance Requirements.   The first step in establishing standards for curriculum objectives is to specify the particular set of outcomes that pertain to the referent situations and to outline the accomplishments that pertain to the outcomes. Table 4-3 provides examples of outcomes and performance requirements associated with three skills in the Homemaking and Community Life Domain that could comprise part of a person's Saturday morning routine: Preparing a Breakfast Meal (H/II I2), Keeping a Kitchen Tidy (H/II A9), and Washing Fabric Items (H/II B2). The outcomes listed in Table 4-3 indicate the characteristics of the environment when performance is completed, and the performance requirements indicate the sequence of accomplishments involved in producing the outcomes. Examples of outcomes and performance requirements for other skills are presented by Gaylord-Ross and Holvoet (1985) and Moon et al. (1985).

Set Criteria.   Once the outcomes and performance requirements are listed, the next step is to set the criteria that apply. Two types of criteria can be used in setting standards: criteria for performance requirements and for outcomes. Criteria for each of these are set in two stages. The first stage is to select the type of measurement system used to quantify the outcomes and performance requirements. It is possible to use any system of measurement that accurately characterizes the outcomes produced—their size, shape, weight, color—or the performance involved in producing the outcomes—the speed, direction, frequency, or timing of the actions. Then the criterion level pertaining to the performance measures is established. This level indicates the point or range in the measurement system that serves to differentiate between acceptable and unacceptable performance. Examples can be found in the activities described in Table 4-3. First, applying criteria to the performance requirements may include determining whether the required ingredients and cookware are assembled; the stove controls used correspond to the burner on which the pot is located and are set to "med-high" or "high" setting; the stove controls are turned off after eggs have boiled for about 5 minutes, etc. Second, applying criteria to the outcomes may include observing whether the eggs seem hard boiled, e.g., neither the egg yolk nor egg white should be "runny"; the toast is light to dark brown; and the juice contains the proportion of juice and water specified on the container of the concentrate.

TABLE 4-3

Outcomes and Performance Requirements for Three Skill Areas: Preparing a Breakfast Meal (H/II I2), Tidying the Kitchen (H/II A9), and Washing Fabric Items (H/II B2)

Settings: Kitchen, dinette, and laundry areas of person's home.
Kitchen is supplied with electric stove, toaster, etc., but does not include a dishwasher.
Laundry area includes a washer and dryer.
The required supplies needed to prepare the breakfast, tidy the kitchen, and wash and dry clothes are available within the setting.

1. *Preparing a Breakfast Meal*

   Outcomes: Two hard boiled eggs, two pieces of toast, and a glass of orange juice, all prepared to the learner's taste.

   Performance Requirements:
   1. Assemble ingredients for hard boiled egg, toast, and orange juice breakfast.
   2. Assemble cookware and serving dishes for the breakfast.
   3. Add eggs and water to pot.
   4. Set stove controls.
   5. Turn off stove controls when eggs are cooked.
   6. Place bread in toaster and engage controls.
   7. Remove bread when toasted and place on plate.
   8. Remove eggs from pot and place on plate.
   9. Pour glass of orange juice.
   10. Place juice, eggs, and toast on table.

2. *Tidying the Kitchen Area*

   Outcomes: Dishes and cookware washed, dried, and returned to storage.
   Food items sealed or wrapped as needed for storage and placed in storage.
   Sink, counter, and table areas washed and free of crumbs, spots, etc.

   Performance Requirements:
   1. Clear dishes from table.
   2. Wash dishes and cookware.
   3. Dry dishes and cookware.
   4. Store leftover and unused ingredients.
   5. Wash table, counter, and sink areas and store cleaning supplies.

3. *Washing Fabric Items*

   Outcomes: Laundry cleaned and free of spots, stains, etc.
   Laundry dried and ready for folding and storage.

   Performance Requirements:
   1. Sort laundry by color/fabric.
   2. Load laundry into washer.
   3. Measure and add detergent.
   4. Engage controls.
   5. Unload clothes from washer when cycle ends.
   6. Load dryer.
   7. Engage controls.
   8. Remove laundry when clothes are dry.

Considerations When Setting Standards

In most instances, the standards used to formulate curriculum objectives should be the same as those that apply to all persons participating in the setting who are of comparable age and social status to the learner (Snell & Browder, 1986). Consequently, the criteria for the outcomes and performance requirements can best be determined by observing the performance of those who are successfully participating in the community setting and by describing the characteristics of the outcomes they produce and the requirements they have met. Likewise, it is useful to interview those who will ultimately apply the standards to the person's performance. For example, family members, friends, and neighbors in domestic settings; employers, supervisors, and fellow workers in work settings; and service personnel and participants (e.g., other shoppers, travelers) in community and leisure settings are all important sources of information in establishing standards for performance (Snell & Smith, 1987).

To ensure that those constructing a curriculum obtain an accurate accounting of the standards that apply in a setting, it is important to follow a formal set of observation guidelines. Certo and Kohl (1984), Easterday and Sitlington (1985), Moon et al. (1985), and others have provided guidelines for determining standards that apply to work settings. These guidelines can pertain to home and community settings as well, and are summarized below:

1. When observing within the setting, allow sufficient time to observe all aspects of performance related to producing the outcomes that are the focus of observation. For example, many outcomes that result from activities such as cooking, cleaning, or participating in leisure activities require preparation before the activity begins and clean-up after the activity ends. These are also part of the performance requirements and must be considered when specifying the standards for curriculum objectives.

2. Transcribe the entire sequence of activities associated with producing the outcomes. It is also useful to note approximate times for beginning and ending steps as well as whether the order of the steps can vary.

3. Indicate any interactions that may occur or are required by persons producing the outcomes. It is important to know the content of any types of communication that may be required as part of producing the outcomes.

4. After making the initial observation, interview the person who will supervise or be involved in performance within the setting. It is advisable to determine where variations in performance can occur and determine minimum performance standards.

5. Perform the observation in a manner as unobtrusive as possible to avoid interrupting or affecting the performance routine or pattern involved in producing the outcomes.

6. Describe the characteristics of the setting that bear upon performance, such as floor plan of a room, equipment and materials used or available for performance, travel routes to and from locations within setting.

Formulating Curriculum Sequences

The final step in constructing a curriculum is to formulate the progressions of curriculum objectives or pathways leading to the endpoints. Completing this step requires (a) determining the prerequisite and lead-up skills that relate to the curriculum endpoints; (b) stating curriculum objectives for the prerequisite and lead-up skills; and (c) organizing the curriculum objectives into curriculum sequences. Upon completing this step, the sequences within the curriculum should permit selection of curriculum objectives for all learners in the instructional programs, including the youngest and the lowest functioning. In addition, the increments between curriculum objectives and the manner in which the objectives are organized should guide the development of individual instructional plans and coordination across instructional units. Thus, the curriculum sequences should facilitate the planning of individual instructional programs that allow learners to progress systematically toward the endpoints of the curriculum, regardless of their current placement and levels of functioning. The age and performance characteristics of the learners are important sources of information in developing sequences of objectives within the curriculum.

Identifying Prerequisite and Lead-up Skills

There are four types of skills that can constitute prerequisite and lead-up skills for the curriculum.

Skills That Represent Subcomponents of the Goal-Related Curriculum Objectives. Many of the objectives for the endpoints of the curriculum require performance of complex patterns or routines. For some of the learners in the instructional programs, it may be neither desirable nor feasible to use the entire routine as the focus of the person's instructional program because of the complexity of the performance required or the level of standards that must be reached. For example, learners served by the agency may not be able to acquire the skills required for preparing a complete meal, following an entire evening hygiene schedule, or completing a day's work assignment when the skills are presented as a single instructional unit. In instances such as these, it is necessary to separate the components of the routine into distinct skills, each of which can become a curriculum objective. For example, with regard to the curriculum objective for preparing a breakfast meal (Table 4-3), separate objectives can be devised for locating and assembling ingredients for the meal, locating and selecting cookware, operating the stove in a safe manner, preparing toast, and so on. If needed, these components can be further subdivided into even less complex skills, and these in turn formulated into curriculum objectives. Table 4-4 provides an example of how a complex skill, such as following a day's work routine, can be divided into component and subcomponent skills.

TABLE 4-4

Breaking Skills into Components and Subcomponents before Devising Curriculum Objectives

Skill: Follows a workday routine

Components:
Subcomponents:

1. Follows check-in procedures
   1.1 Enters building and goes to employee locker area
   1.2 Stores lunch and changes into work clothes
   1.3 Procures safety gear
   1.4 Reports to employee check-in area

2. Completes work preparation at work station
   2.1 Greets supervisor and fellow workers
   2.2 Procures supplies needed for workday
   2.3 Checks operation of equipment

3. Follows morning work routine
   3.1 Operates equipment in safe manner
   3.2 Checks products for defects
   3.3 Stacks and packages completed products
   3.4 Follows employee break routine at designated time

4. Follows employee lunch routine
   4.1 Returns to locker room, gathers lunch and belongings, and goes to cafeteria
   4.2 Follows lunch routine
   4.3 Displays mealtime etiquette
   4.4 Tidies eating area
   4.5 Returns lunch pail and belongings to locker and returns to work station

5. Follows afternoon work routines
   5.1 Completes 3.1-3.4 above
   5.2 Tidies work area at end of shift

6. Follows check-out procedures
   6.1 Leaves work area
   6.2 Secures safety gear
   6.3 Changes into street clothes
   6.4 Leaves building

Skills That Represent Performance in Simulated Settings and Situations. Curriculum objectives can also be devised to guide instruction in simulated settings or situations (Lakin & Bruininks, 1985). Doing so involves developing objectives in which the conditions of performance, the performance requirements, or the standards are modified in a way that does *not* precisely correspond to those encountered in the natural environment. For example, curriculum objectives can be developed to prepare learners to perform a shopping routine after store hours, complete work activities at stations created in the agency rather than in the community, or select clothing items to fit the occasion through use of instructional aids instead of the learner's clothes.

Preparing curriculum objectives for simulated settings and situations permits a greater refinement or breakdown of objectives than can be achieved by dividing complex skills into subcomponents. For example, objectives may permit the instructor to control the conditions for performance to reduce the number of extraneous variables learners may encounter. Other objectives may have standards less stringent than those found in natural circumstances so that learners can produce outcomes and thereby maintain interest in the instructional activities. As a consequence, such objectives can facilitate intensive instruction, allow repeated practice of specific skills, permit easy error correction as the need arises, reduce the requirements for instructional time and resources, and enhance general case learning (Horner, McDonnell, & Bellamy, 1986; Nietupski, Hamre-Nietupski, Clancy, & Veerhusen, 1986).

Even with these advantages, those constructing curricula should be cautious in formulating objectives using simulated situations and settings as referents. For example, there is little evidence to show that simulation is an effective instructional approach with learners who are low functioning (Horner, McDonnell, & Bellamy, 1986). When curriculum objectives based on simulation are included in the curriculum, it is essential that additional objectives be developed to ensure transfer and generalization of the skills to the circumstances learners will actually encounter in the community.

Skills That Are Prerequisite to Goal-Related Performance. Before persons can participate effectively in many community settings, they must be able to exhibit a minimum level of performance in such areas as communication, cognition, motor control, and social interaction (Guess, 1980; Meyer & Evans, 1986; Reichle & Keogh, 1986; White, 1980). For example, participation in most work settings requires persons to exhibit sufficient stamina and strength to get through the workday and to have enough balance and coordination to operate the equipment or manipulate the materials associated with the work assignment. Similar requirements will also pertain to skills in the Homemaking and Community Life, Travel, and Leisure domains. For those persons who lack prerequisite skills, it is necessary to include curriculum objectives designed to develop them. These objectives must be contained within the agency curriculum.

The best sources of information for identifying prerequisite skills are the curriculum guides and assessment devices that are community-referenced and developed for learners having comparable characteristics to those served by the agency. Some of the many sources for selecting prerequisite skills are Functional Speech and Language Training for the Severely Handicapped (Guess, Sailor, & Baer, 1976), the Adaptive Behavior Curriculum (Popovich & Laham, 1981), VOCSKILLS (Vocational Opportunities Cooperative, 1982), and Independent Living Skills Curriculum (Taylor, Close, Carlson, & Larrabee, 1981). It is important to emphasize, however, that guides such as these should be used only as resources and may, in fact, be of very limited use in constructing an agency curriculum. The endpoints of the agency curriculum should continue to serve as the referents for establishing curriculum objectives. The skills selected from commercially developed instruments should be limited to those constituting prerequisites to the endpoints. Unless the goals and endpoints serve as a guide throughout the process of constructing a curriculum, it is likely that the instructional programs that result from an agency curriculum will not be consistent or continuous.

Skills That Facilitate the Instructional Process.   There are many skills that increase the effectiveness and efficiency of instruction for learners who display them. Included among these are attentiveness to instructional activities, ability to imitate the actions of other people, compliance with directions, initiating actions and interactions, and many others (Knapczyk, 1983; Knapczyk, Johnson, & McDermott, 1983; Meyer & Evans, 1986; Wacker & Hoffman, 1984). Research has repeatedly demonstrated that learners who display such skills benefit from instruction to a greater degree than do those who do not display such skills (Reichle & Keogh, 1986). To identify the skills most pertinent to the learners in the agency's program, those constructing a curriculum are encouraged to examine research studies that investigate the relationship between learning characteristics and skill acquisition published in professional journals. In some instances, skills that facilitate instruction can be developed in community settings and the curriculum objectives devised for the skills should reflect the conditions of performance and standards for these settings (Donnellan & Neel, 1986; Meyer & Evans, 1986). In other instances, simulated or controlled settings will have to serve as referents for the objectives (Horner, McDonnell, & Bellamy, 1986).

The need to consider these types of skills in identifying prerequisite and lead-up skills will be determined by the characteristics of the persons in the instructional programs. For example, agencies providing instruction to young children or persons with severe physical impairments or behavioral disorders may have to develop extensive lists of curriculum objectives for those skills prerequisite to goal-related performance and those that facilitate instruction. Agencies providing instruction to learners who are older or higher functioning can usually concentrate on developing objectives for goal-related performance and their subcomponents and objectives for simulated settings and situations (Sailor et al., 1986).

Stating Curriculum Objectives for Prerequisite and Lead-up Skills

The curriculum objectives for prerequisite and lead-up skills should follow the same format used for devising objectives for the goal-related endpoints. Each objective should describe the skills that will be the focus of instruction; indicate the conditions (i.e., setting and situations) under which the skills will be exhibited; and specify the standards that must be met to produce the desired outcomes. The skills described in the objectives should closely correspond to the performance that persons must display to participate successfully in community settings. In addition, the conditions of performance and the standards in the objectives should correspond to those that persons will encounter in these settings.

In specifying objectives for the curriculum, attention should also be given to the increments between the objectives. An increment represents the amount of time required by learners to progress from one curriculum objective to the next one in the sequence. For example, curriculum objectives can be devised so that learners can progress from one objective to the next in a short period of time, such as 1 or 2 weeks. However, the smaller the increment between objectives, the greater the total number of objectives the curriculum will contain. For agencies providing instruction to learners with diverse characteristics, it is possible to develop so many objectives that the curriculum becomes unusable. For example, it may become impossible for the instructors to sort through the items in the curriculum to find the set of objectives suitable for specific learners. Curriculum objectives can also be devised with large increments between them, such as several years. In this instance a large amount of instruction will be required before any single objective is attained. However, when increments between objectives are too large, they do not serve as useful guides for planning individual instructional programs and can hamper consistency and continuity of instruction across instructional units. As a general rule, those constructing a curriculum should devise objectives to represent increments of about 6 to 10 months, or to correspond to the individual instructional planning or review process used by the agency. That is, the objectives contained in the curriculum should enhance evaluation of existing program plans and facilitate selection of more advanced objectives for the learners.

Thus, when developing curriculum objectives for prerequisites and lead-up skills, those engaged in constructing a curriculum must project the amount of progress learners within the instructional program can be expected to make between program planning sessions based upon their learning characteristics.

Organizing Curriculum Objectives into Curriculum Sequences

The objectives contained in the agency curriculum must be organized to permit easy and efficient access to them during the instructional planning process. That is, after assessing the current functioning level of the learners, the instructional staff should be able to quickly locate sets of curriculum objectives suitable for the learners' program plans. Cataloging curriculum objectives according to two levels of organization will enhance the usefulness of the curriculum during the planning of instructional programs.

Organizing Objectives by Instructional Goals. The first level of organization requires grouping the objectives according to the instructional goals of the agency. The system of organization provided by the taxonomy provides a useful guide for doing this. The curriculum objectives are first grouped according to each of the domains, then according to the endpoints, and finally according to the skill areas that constitute the goals of the agency curriculum. This level of organization can greatly reduce overlap and duplication of instructional services across the instructional units of an agency. For example, sets of interrelated curriculum objectives that form sections of the curriculum can be assigned to each of the instructional units. In instances where overlap or duplication of objectives exists, objectives can be specifically assigned to one of the units, or procedures can be devised for coordinating instructional activities across the units. For example, an agency providing instructional services to adults may assign the objectives that pertain to traveling from home to work in the morning to the Home Living unit and those that pertain to traveling home after the workday to the Vocational unit. Procedures can then be devised by the staff to ensure that instructional activities are consistent across the two units.

For curricula that contain objectives for many prerequisite and lead-up skills, it is likely that comparable objectives will be grouped under more than one domain or endpoint. Objectives in such areas as communication, mobility, and social interaction pertain to many of the endpoints in the Travel, Leisure, and Vocational domains, and should be assigned accordingly. In some instances objectives for prerequisite and lead-up skills may be organized as distinct objectives in order to highlight unique features in the conditions of performance or standards that apply to a setting or situation. For example, objectives for the same mobility skills may be grouped across several endpoints because characteristics in home, community, and vocational settings require that different performance requirements must be met within each of them. For other skills, curriculum objectives can be organized to reflect a general case programming approach to facilitate flexible and adaptable performance across an array of settings and situations. Curricula developed in specific content areas, such as those devised by Dever (1978), MacDonald and Horstmeier (1978), Wessel (1979), and others can provide very useful resources for organizing curriculum objectives that apply across domains. Guidelines developed by Horner, McDonnell, and Bellamy (1986) also can be helpful in organizing objectives such as these. In either case, it is essential that the manner through which objectives for prerequisite and lead-up skills are organized within the curriculum facilitates coordinated and consistent planning across the instructional units.

Organizing Objectives by Difficulty.   The second level of organization requires sequencing objectives by difficulty. Such an ordering will facilitate the selection of specific objectives from among the range of objectives pertaining to each of the endpoints and skills. For example, once a learner has demonstrated mastery of one objective in a curriculum area, instructional personnel should be able to use the curriculum to identity the next objective along the continuum that progresses toward the endpoint or goal.

Performance requirements associated with the settings in which performance is to occur provide a base for sequencing objectives by level of difficulty. For example, objectives that correspond to components and subcomponents of performance routines and patterns can be sequenced by the degree of complexity or contiguity of the actions comprising the routine. Those that are more complex or that require greater contiguity of action should be sequenced after those requiring less complexity and less contiguity. Objectives for prerequisite skills by their very nature must be organized sequentially because instruction in the more advanced skills will not be effective until the basic skills are achieved. Objectives for skills that facilitate participation in instructional programs can be incorporated into the curriculum at the points at which these skills become essential to implementation of instructional activities. Objectives devised for skills displayed in simulated settings or situations can also be organized sequentially according to the degree to which they represent the conditions and standards within the natural settings. Those objectives that most closely approximate performance in the natural environment should be sequenced after those that represent a greater disparity from the natural environment.

After the curriculum objectives have been formulated and sequenced, it is useful to devise a system for cataloging objectives so that the instructional staff can easily access them when planning instructional programs. Adopting and extending the cataloging system used within the taxonomy, that is, using letters to designate the domains and roman numerals, letters, and two-digit numbers to represent headings, subheadings, etc., can provide an effective method of organizing objectives in the curriculum.

CONCLUDING STATEMENT

Constructing curricula must be a major and ongoing program planning activity for agencies that provide instruction to persons who are low functioning. The curriculum devised by an agency must suit the specific needs of the persons receiving instructional services and must represent clearly the requirements of the community in which the persons live. In addition, the curriculum must reflect that agency's mission within the community and its access to resources that support instructional programs. To achieve these ends, it is apparent that constructing a curriculum must be viewed as a complex process, requiring attention to many factors. A resource guide such as this taxonomy can provide valuable assistance in examining those factors that relate directly to the process of constructing a curriculum.

The taxonomy provides a framework agencies can use to formulate and operationalize the goals of the instructional programs. It also provides a community template or reference system that curriculum developers can use to obtain information about the learners, the community, and the agency and to incorporate the information into the curriculum objectives. Finally, it offers a system of organization by which instructional pathways leading to the instructional goals of the agency can be devised. Used as a referent, the taxonomy can increase the efficiency of whatever process an agency uses to construct a curriculum and can enhance the quality of the curriculum that results.

It is important to note that constructing a curriculum is but one facet of the instructional paradigm (see Figure 2-1). Once an agency has devised a curriculum, there are many additional factors the staff must consider in planning quality instructional services for persons who are low functioning. Developing procedures for assessing the current level of functioning with regard to the objectives, task analysis of curriculum objectives to fit the unique learning characteristics of each learner, and creating activities that are instructional and motivating for learners within individual and group arrangements are only some of the other factors that affect the quality of instructional programs. Recently, much attention has been given to these aspects of the instructional paradigm in the professional literature (e.g., Horner, Meyer, & Fredericks, 1986; Liberty, 1985; Snell, 1987). It is through such efforts that the basic goals of community-referenced programming can be achieved.

Section II

Taxonomy of Community Living Skills

Chapter 5

Domain P
Personal Maintenance and Development

Independent people take care of themselves: they keep their bodies clean, they take care of their clothing and personal effects, they maintain their health, etc. And when their bodies have problems they provide care, either by themselves or with medical assistance. In addition, if all goes well they live in a family context and make friends. Both must be nurtured to endure. Finally, independent persons also find that Murphy's Law is constantly in effect: that is, "If anything can go wrong, it will." Therefore, they must respond to the glitches that show up in everyday life. They range from the shampoo bottle that is found empty after beginning the shower to the sleepless night that leaves one tired the next day.

P/I: GOALS RELATED TO
ROUTINE BODY MAINTENANCE

For two reasons it is important for all of us to maintain our bodies in good condition: Good physical condition allows us to perform and continue to perform in the best way possible, and it is necessary to develop both strength, agility, and endurance, and general health. Second, it is in order to get by in our culture without attracting negative attention, one should present the best possible appearance to others, including dress, bodily cleanliness, neatness in grooming, and posture. In each of these areas, many low-functioning people have difficulties. An inordinate number are in woeful physical condition, and too many present an inappropriate appearance to the world. Neither condition works to their advantage. It is a reality that some people must seem more normal than normal just to be allowed to melt into the crowd. Therefore, establishing and maintaining good physical condition and appearance are both very important.

P/I A: The Learner Will Maintain Personal Cleanliness

One of the more important areas of personal maintenance is that of personal cleanliness. The person who keeps his body and clothing clean will be able to enter more situations than one who is dirty and smells bad. Therefore, personal cleanliness is a major area of instruction for persons who must live in the community.

1. Bathe
   1.01 Shower/bath
   1.02 Hands/face

2. Shampoo hair

3. Brush/floss teeth

4. Maintain clothing cleanliness

5. Care for menses (females)

6. Clean nails
   6.01 Fingernails
   6.02 Toenails

7. Clean nose
   7.01 Colds, allergies, etc.
   7.02 Dust, dirt
   7.03 Other

8. Eliminate waste

9. Care for skin

10. Other

P/I B: The Learner Will Groom Self

Grooming is also very important for people who must learn to live in the community. The person who is well groomed will not only be allowed to go more places and do more things than will one who is not, he or she will also be perceived as being more competent. Therefore, while matters such as teaching females to shave their underarms may be perceived as inappropriate by some social theorists, in a practical sense, it must be done: the greater the difficulty a person has becoming integrated into the community, the more it is necessary to teach that person to present his or her physical self in the best possible light.

1. Keep hair trimmed and neat
   1.01 Barber (males)
   1.02 Hair stylist (females)

2. Comb/brush hair

3. Shave
   3.01 Face (males)
   3.02 Legs and underarms (females)

4. Trim nails
   4.01 Fingers
   4.02 Toes
   4.03 Cuticles

5. Use deodorant

6. Use makeup (females)

7. Other

P/I C: The Learner Will Dress Appropriately

Clothing contributes to a major part of one's appearance. It is important to attend not only to the type of clothing one wears, but also to the manner in which one wears it. Many low-functioning persons live on limited budgets, and food and shelter may take priority over fashionable clothing purchases. Nevertheless, even people on limited budgets can learn to look neat if they are taught to select and wear appropriate clothing. For example, retarded people who have sufficient funds should learn never to "dress retarded." Dressing appropriately also includes the selection of specific clothing to fit both location and weather conditions. ·

1. Maintain neatness in clothing
   1.01 Fit
   1.02 Adjustment
   1.03 Cleanliness
        1.03.01 Wash
        1.03.02 Dry clean
        1.03.03 Brush
        1.03.04 Other
   1.04 Storage procedures
        1.04.01 Daily
        1.04.02 Seasonal
        1.04.03 Other

2. Maintain shoes
   2.01 Fit
   2.02 Wear
   2.03 Cleanliness

3. Observe local clothing style(s)

4. Coordinate clothing colors and patterns

5. Wear appropriate clothing for activities
   5.01 Formal
   5.02 Sports
   5.03 Work
   5.04 Leisure
   5.05 Other

6. Wear clothing appropriate to location
   6.01 Indoors/outdoors
   6.02 Formal/informal
   6.03 Other

7. Wear clothing appropriate for weather
  7.01 Temperature/humidity
  7.02 Precipitation
  7.03 Wind factors
  7.04 Change wet clothing
  7.05 Other

8. Repair or discard worn clothing

9. Discard out-of-style clothing

10. Other

P/I D: The Learner Will Maintain Appropriate Sleep Patterns

Another illness prevention pattern is getting appropriate amounts of sleep. While it is true that some people need less sleep than others, everyone needs some. Those who do not get the sleep they need will pay the price in reduced effectiveness in their jobs and the other things they must do. They also run the risk of developing debilitating illnesses.

1. Identify required sleep patterns
  1.01 Learner's physical requirements
  1.02 External factors
      1.02.01 Job schedule
      1.02.02 Chore schedule
      1.02.03 Activity schedule
      1.02.04 Other

2. Follow required sleep pattern
  2.01 Bedtime/arising time
  2.02 Alarm clocks/radios
  2.03 Other

P/I E: The Learner Will Maintain Nutrition

Maintaining nutrition is more than a matter of eating regularly: it requires balancing one's diet in order to keep one's body as healthy as possible. It involves eating the right things, avoiding the wrong things, and monitoring the quantity of food ingested.

1. Eat balanced meals
   1.01 Meats
   1.02 Dairy
   1.03 Breads
   1.04 Fruits

2. Maintain appropriate body weight
   2.01 Maximum/minimum weight targets
   2.02 Food quantity
        2.02.01 Meals
        2.02.02 Snacks

P/I F: The Learner Will Exercise Regularly

Regular exercise is known to benefit everyone. While few low-functioning people will become recognized athletes (although it *does* happen), most can participate in some form of regular exercise, whether it be walking, swimming, calisthenics, or some other form. Such exercise is important to the maintenance of health, endurance, and vigor.

1. Exercise cardiovascular system

2. Exercise skeletal muscle system

P/I G: The Learner Will Maintain Substance Control

One of the most potentially devastating problems for anyone is loss of personal control because of drug or alcohol abuse. The effects on the body and mind can be terrible. It is important to teach low-functioning persons (just as it is to teach anyone) to control the use of such dangerous substances.

1. Control use of dangerous substances
    1.01 Drugs
    1.02 Alcohol
    1.03 Tobacco
    1.04 Other

2. Seek assistance if substance use is out of control

P/II: GOALS RELATED TO
ILLNESS TREATMENT

Everyone gets injured or ill occasionally. When necessary, illness and injury must be treated in some fashion. Sometimes illnesses and injuries are minor and can be treated by the person himself, but at other times the problem is of such a nature that medical assistance is required. Low-functioning persons must learn the difference between self-treatable and other problems, and what to do about illness or injury when it strikes.

P/II A: The Learner Will Use Appropriate First Aid and Illness Treatment Procedures

First aid is basic to independence. Learners must know what to do about minor injuries and illnesses ranging from small cuts and scrapes to head colds and flu.

1. Identify injuries requiring first aid
    1.01 Minor cuts
    1.02 Scrapes
    1.03 Splinters
    1.04 Sprains
    1.05 Burns
    1.06 Minor illnesses
    1.07 Occasional headache
    1.08 Other

2. Treat minor injuries

3. Maintain first aid supplies

4. Identify illness requiring home treatment
    4.01 Colds
    4.02 Flu
    4.03 Other

5. Other

P/II B: The Learner Will Obtain Medical Advice and Treatment When Necessary

The difference between major and minor illness or injury is often apparent, but sometimes it is not. Headaches, for example, may be the simple byproduct of a head cold or they may indicate serious internal problems. If for no reason other than the fact that it is less expensive to treat as many problems as possible at home, it is necessary to learn to distinguish between those problems that require medical assistance and those that do not. It is also necessary to learn to follow routine procedures such as making appointments for periodic checkups in order to prevent serious physical problems from developing.

1. Identify injury or illness requiring medical intervention
   1.01 Cuts
   1.02 Burns
   1.03 Sprains
   1.04 Broken bones
   1.05 Pain
   1.06 Illness
   1.07 Other

2. Follow emergency procedures when appropriate
   2.01 Emergency Medical Service (EMS)
   2.02 Emergency telephone numbers
   2.03 Physician
   2.04 Dentist
   2.05 Other

3. Follow routine procedures when appropriate
   3.01 Periodic examinations
       3.01.01 Physician
       3.01.02 Dentist
       3.01.03 Optometrist
       3.01.04 Other
   3.02 Minor illnesses

P/II C: The Learner Will Follow Required Medication Schedules

When medicine is prescribed, the schedule must be adhered to or it may not benefit (and could possibly harm) the learner. The reason is that medicines vary: some must be taken once a day, some more often; some must be taken with food, some on an empty stomach; and some interact positively or negatively with others if taken simultaneously. Because they tend to take more medication than most people, low-functioning learners must learn to follow medication schedules.

1. Obtain prescription for medication
   1.01 Amount
   1.02 Frequency
   1.03 Termination
   1.04 Other

2. Follow prescribed course of medication

P/III: GOALS RELATED TO ESTABLISHING AND MAINTAINING PERSONAL RELATIONSHIPS

Establishing and maintaining relationships with family and friends is important because these relationships are fundamental to human existence. Unfortunately, our close relationships are not always pleasant. Family life, for example, can be hellish (as is the case when relatives are physically or mentally abusive). In such cases, it may be important for learners to learn how to get assistance. Similarly, the right friendships can make life pleasant, but the wrong ones can cause great difficulty, as is the case when one's "friends" are either unfriendly or nonexistent. Therefore, it is necessary not only to learn to make friends, but also to make the right friends.

P/III A: The Learner Will Interact Appropriately With Family

The family is usually thought of as the center of our society. For many people this idea is reality, but for many others it is not. Some people do not have families at all, while others have families that are full of hatred and pain. Nevertheless, family ties are often strong, and low-functioning persons must learn to handle whatever relationships exist in a productive manner. It should be noted that each person in a family is required not only to interact in certain ways (e.g., to play the role of parent or child), but also *not* to interact in certain ways (e.g., refrain from incestual relationships). In addition, familial relationships can change (e.g., low-functioning persons can develop families of their own). If they do, they will have a different set of relationships to maintain than is the case when they play the role of son, daughter, or sibling.

1. Perform required interactions
   1.01 Parents/guardians
   1.02 Siblings
   1.03 Spouse
   1.04 Children
   1.05 Other

2. Refrain from interacting inappropriately

3. Observe demeanor requirements within family
   3.01 Deference
   3.02 Familiarity
   3.03 Assertiveness
   3.04 Other

4. Observe conversational constraints within family

5. Make appropriate response to emotions of family

6. Make appropriate emotional responses to family members

7. Display appropriate body language
   7.01 Posture
   7.02 Facial expressions
   7.03 Gestures
   7.04 Movements
   7.05 Other

P/III B: The Learner Will Make Friends

Friends are important and recent data indicate that many low-functioning persons lack friends: they may go to school or work, but then many come home and sit. Perhaps one of the reasons so many people in this group lack friends is that they have not been taught how to make friends.

1. Identify potential friends
   1.01 Same sex
   1.02 Opposite sex

2. Make appropriate overtures

3. Make friends

P/III C: The Learner Will Interact Appropriately With Friends

Once friendships have been made, they must be maintained. Sometimes it can be difficult to continue to interact in a positive manner, but maintaining appropriate friendships is often worth the effort.

1. Observe required interactions
   1.01 Same sex
   1.02 Opposite sex

2. Refrain from interacting inappropriately

3. Observe demeanor requirements
   3.01 Deference
   3.02 Familiarity
   3.03 Assertiveness
   3.04 Other

4. Observe conversational constraints with friends

5. Make appropriate response to emotions of friends

6. Make appropriate emotional responses to friends

7. Display appropriate body language
   7.01 Posture
   7.02 Facial expressions
   7.03 Gestures
   7.04 Movements
   7.05 Other

P/III D: The Learner Will Respond to Inappropriate Conduct of Family and Friends

Sadly, many persons, including low-functioning persons, will experience inappropriate conduct on the part of others who are close to them. In extreme cases, such conduct may consist of physical and mental abuse, including neglect and sexual abuse. Those who experience inappropriate conduct must be able to respond to it before it affects them too greatly.

1. Identify inappropriate conduct of others
   1.01 Exploitation
   1.02 Manipulation
   1.03 Harassment
   1.04 Teasing
   1.05 Incest
   1.06 Physical abuse
   1.07 Neglect
   1.08 Fighting
   1.09 Other

2. Respond to inappropriate conduct of family members and friends
   2.01 Seek assistance
      2.01.01 Friends
      2.01.02 Neighbors
      2.01.03 Officials
   2.02 Leave area
   2.03 Defend self
   2.04 Other

P/III E: The Learner Will Respond Acceptably to Sexual Needs

Like anyone else, low-functioning persons can have active sexual lives. Those who are able to be active sexually have the right to do so if they so choose. Sexual activity, however, is socially constrained, and breaking the rules will bring negative attention. Therefore, learners must be taught to express their sexuality in socially acceptable ways.

1. Identify sexual needs
2. Respond appropriately to social constraints when satisfying sexual needs
   2.01 Sexual partners
   2.02 Masturbation
   2.03 Birth control
   2.04 Other

P/III F: The Learner Will Obtain Necessary Assistance in Maintaining Relationships With Family and Friends

Any personal relationship can end, and sadness and pain accompany loss of friendships or loving relationships. If the pain is great enough, it may be necessary to obtain outside assistance.

1. Identify problems in personal relationships
   1.01 Strained relationships
        1.01.01 Quarrels
        1.01.02 Separation
        1.01.03 Other
   1.02 Loss of relationship
        1.02.01 Death
        1.02.02 Divorce
        1.02.03 Quarrels
        1.02.04 Other
2. Obtain assistance in coping with personal problems
   2.01 Family
   2.02 Friends
   2.03 Professionals
   2.04 Other

P/IV: GOALS RELATED
TO THE HANDLING OF
GLITCHES

As in each of the domains, things can and do go wrong in our personal lives. Everyone gets surprised when schedules change, equipment breaks, or supplies run out. Whatever happens, low-functioning persons must learn to handle the ups and downs associated with their personal lives.

P/IV A: The Learner Will Cope With Changes in Daily Schedule(s)

Changes in scheduled activities can be very disruptive to low-functioning persons. Maintaining personal balance is partly a matter of coping with such disruptions.

1. Cope with sleep pattern disruptions
   1.01 Insomnia
   1.02 Activity induced
   1.03 Schedule changes
   1.04 Emergencies
   1.05 Other

2. Cope with the result of sleep pattern disruptions
   2.01 Fatigue
   2.02 Irritability
   2.03 Next day activities
   2.04 Other

3. Perform alternate activities during changes in daily routine(s)
   3.01 Holidays
   3.02 Weather days
   3.03 Emergencies
   3.04 Other

P/IV B: The Learner Will Cope With Equipment Breakdowns or Materials Depletions

As much as anyone tries to maintain appropriate supplies, it seems that the shampoo always runs out after one's hair is good and wet. It is necessary to learn to cope with such events.

1. Repair or replace broken equipment
   1.01 Grooming
   1.02 Personal cleanliness

2. Replace depleted materials
   2.01 Grooming
   2.02 Personal cleanliness
   2.03 Other

3. Perform alternate activities

Chapter 6

Domain H
Homemaking and
Community Life

People who are independent are community members: they blend into their neighborhoods and do not draw negative attention to themselves. They take care of their living quarters in much the same way as do those around them, they feed themselves and pay rent, etc. They also get along with most of the neighbors, the local merchants and service personnel, the police, and other officials. Therefore, the goals listed in the domain of Homemaking and Community Life are those pertaining to finding and caring for one's living quarters, getting along with the neighbors and others in the community, and handling the glitches that arise during daily community life.

H/I: GOALS RELATED TO
OBTAINING LIVING QUARTERS

An independent person finds it necessary to change living quarters from time to time. For any number of reasons people must move from one place to another: they may change jobs, or the landlord may sell the building. For whatever the reason, when the time comes to move, the learner must be ready to handle it. Moving is a complicated event, however, and many learners will require a great deal of instruction before they are ready to do it without assistance.

H/I A: The Learner Will Find Appropriate Living Quarters

The first thing a person must do to move to new living quarters is to find a place to live. To do this, it is necessary to assess the suitability of potential living quarters, a problem with many dimensions. Most people, for example, soon discover that many places in which it would be *nice* to live have problems: they are too expensive, or they are in the wrong location, etc. Moving into such a place, no matter how nice it may be, would be a mistake, and another place must be found. In addition, while some persons prefer to live alone, many people want to have roommates/housemates or will have spouses and/or children who must take part in the decision. To be successful at living independently, learners must learn to make judgments that take factors such as these into account.

1. Locate potential quarters
   1.01 Formal networks
      1.01.01 Newspaper ads
      1.01.02 Real estate agents
      1.01.03 Other
   1.02 Informal networks
      1.02.01 Family
      1.02.02 Friends/acquaintances
      1.02.03 Other

2. Assess desirability of potential living quarters
   2.01 Location
   2.02 Cost
   2.03 Roommates/housemates
   2.04 Family considerations
   2.05 Physical plant
      2.05.01 Physical barriers
      2.05.02 Physical aids
      2.05.03 Equipment
      2.05.04 Furnishings
      2.05.05 Other
   2.06 Availability of services
      2.06.01 Stores
      2.06.02 Medical
      2.06.03 Transportation
      2.06.04 Recreation
      2.06.05 Other

3. Assess ability to pay costs
   3.01 Income
   3.02 Expenses
   3.03 Others to share costs
   3.04 Other

H/I B: The Learner Will Rent/Buy Living Quarters

The act of selecting and moving into living quarters requires an agreement with someone else, such as the landlord or the seller. The learner must learn how to make such agreements.

1. Select living quarters

2. Agree on price

3. Sign agreements
   3.01 Landlord
   3.02 Roommates/housemates

4. Make deposit(s)

5. Budget costs

H/I C: The Learner Will Set Up Living Quarters

Once a person finds a place to live and decides to move in, there are many things to do. Chief among them is the fact that the new place must be stocked and furnished (unless, of course, it comes furnished).

1. Obtain needed furniture
2. Obtain food, tools, and materials
3. Move
   3.01 Pack belongings
   3.02 Obtain transportation
   3.03 Move
4. Set up furniture
5. Store food, tools, and materials

H/II: GOALS RELATED TO
COMMUNITY LIFE ROUTINES

Anyone who lives in an independent living situation must care for the living quarters, make arrangements to eat, and pay the bills. To name just a few of the things that must be done: the quarters must be kept clean, light bulbs must be changed, sidewalks cleared of snow, repairs must be made, the food supply must be replenished and food prepared.

H/II A: The Learner Will Keep Living Quarters Neat and Clean

Keeping living quarters clean is time consuming. There are many things to do and they must be done on various schedules. For example, the beds are usually made every day, but refrigerators need defrosting only a couple of times each year. Learners must learn not only *how* to clean up, but also *when* to do so.

1. Vacuum each room at appropriate times
   1.01 Floors
   1.02 Baseboards
   1.03 Curtains
   1.04 Other

2. Dust/sweep each room at appropriate times
   2.01 Furniture
   2.02 Corners
   2.03 Other

3. Wash surfaces at appropriate times
   3.01 Floors
   3.02 Fixtures
   3.03 Interior windows
   3.04 Tiles
   3.05 Porcelain
   3.06 Formica
   3.07 Other

4. Dampwipe surfaces at appropriate times
   4.01 Appliances
   4.02 Fixtures
   4.03 Countertops
   4.04 Other

5. Wash metal furniture parts as required

6. Clean and/or polish wood at appropriate times
   6.01 Furniture
   6.02 Cabinets
   6.03 Floors
   6.04 Wall paneling
   6.05 Other

7. Defrost refrigerator/freezer at appropriate times

8. Clean oven at appropriate times

9. Keep rooms tidy relative to clutter
   9.01 Accumulation
   9.02 Spills
   9.03 Make beds

10. Tidy storage areas as required
    10.01 Closets
    10.02 Cabinets
    10.03 Dressers
    10.04 Kitchen drawers
    10.05 Other

11. Store cleaning supplies after use
    11.01 Full/partially full
    11.02 Empties

12. Remove waste at appropriate times

13. Replace cleaning materials as required
    13.01 Periodic inventory
    13.02 Purchase
    13.03 Store

14. Other

H/II B: The Learner Will Keep Fabric Items Clean and Repaired

Most homes have machines to wash linens and other fabrics, but furniture and rugs often require special cleaning crews and some fabrics must be dry cleaned. In addition, both clean and dirty fabrics must be stored and sometimes mended.

1. Store dirty fabrics
   1.01 Linens
   1.02 Towels
   1.03 Clothing
   1.04 Other

2. Wash fabrics on appropriate schedule
   2.01 Clothing
   2.02 Linens
   2.03 Towels
   2.04 Carpets
   2.05 Furniture
   2.06 Other

3. Store clean fabrics
   3.01 Clothing
   3.02 Linens
   3.03 Towels
   3.04 Other

4. Repair or mend fabrics as required

5. Replace fabrics as required

6. Store supplies after use
   6.01 Cleaning
   6.02 Repair
   6.03 Other

H/II C: The Learner Will Maintain Interior of Living Quarters

Everyone who moves into his own place soon discovers that light bulbs burn out, soap and cleaning fluids get used up, and appliances become dysfunctional. If maintenance is not performed on these things, the learner will soon live in a nonfunctional environment. Therefore, it is necessary to learn to maintain the interior of the living quarters.

1. Paint surfaces as required
   1.01 Floors
   1.02 Walls
   1.03 Ceilings
   1.04 Moldings
   1.05 Other

2. Repair or replace household equipment as required
   2.01 Consumables
           2.01.01 Light bulbs
           2.01.02 Fuses
           2.01.03 Other
   2.02 Tools
           2.02.01 Cleaning
           2.02.02 Repair
           2.02.03 Other
   2.03 Fixtures
   2.04 Appliances

3. Replace maintenance supplies as required
   3.01 Inventory supplies
           3.01.01 Soap/cleaning fluid
           3.01.02 Toilet paper
   3.02 Purchase supplies
   3.03 Discard empty containers

H/II D: The Learner Will Maintain the Exterior of Living Quarters

Not only is it necessary to maintain the interior of the living quarters, it is often necessary to care for the yard and the exterior of the home. If one lives in an apartment, the landlord will often do the work, but if one lives in a separate home, the resident gets stuck with it. Therefore, like everyone else, low-functioning people must learn to do what must be done to maintain neighborhood standards.

1. Keep debris from accumulating
   1.01 Trash/garbage
   1.02 Debris
   1.03 Other

2. Wash exterior surfaces on appropriate schedule
   2.01 Windows
   2.02 Storm fixtures
   2.03 Other

3. Change storm doors and windows on appropriate schedule

4. Store outdoor furniture and equipment on appropriate schedule

5. Repair outdoor furniture, equipment, and fixtures as required

6. Tend plants
   6.01 Lawns
   6.02 Shrubs
   6.03 Flowers
   6.04 Vegetable garden
   6.05 Other

7. Keep walks and drives clear of ice and snow

8. Maintain and repair exterior structure of building
   8.01 Painted surfaces
   8.02 Unpainted surfaces
   8.03 Structural problems

9. Other

H/II E: The Learner Will Respond to Seasonal Changes

As the seasons change we must make adjustments to our living quarters. Storm windows must be put on (or taken down); the furnace must be cleaned or shut off; yard chores must be completed, etc.

1. Respond to temperature changes
   1.01 Heating/air conditioning
   1.02 Storm windows/screens

2. Respond to chore change requirements
   2.01 Grass/snow
   2.02 Seasonal cleaning chores
   2.03 Other

H/II F: The Learner Will Follow Home Safety Procedures

Safety in the home is something everyone must learn in order to survive. Fires must be prevented, procedures must be followed for changing light bulbs, and things that can cause one to lose one's footing must be picked up off the floor.

1. Prevent fires
   1.01 Material storage
   1.02 Flammables use
   1.03 Other

2. Prevent accidents
   2.01 Material use and storage
   2.02 Tool use and storage
   2.03 Slippery surfaces
   2.04 Heights
   2.05 Other

3. Other

H/II G: The Learner Will Follow Accident/Emergency Procedures

Emergencies do not often arise, but when they do, learners must be prepared to handle them.

1. Identify accident/emergency
    1.01 Weather
        1.01.01 Storms
        1.01.02 Excessive precipitation
    1.02 Fire
    1.03 Personal injury
        1.03.01 Self
        1.03.02 Other person
    1.04 Other

2. Respond to accident/emergency
    2.01 Inform responsible party
        2.01.01 Police
        2.01.02 Local emergency number
        2.01.03 Paramedics
        2.01.04 Fire department
        2.01.05 Repair personnel
        2.01.06 Other
    2.02 Make personal response
        2.02.01 Storms
                2.02.01.01 Secure building
                2.02.01.02 Evacuation
                2.02.01.03 Seek shelter
                2.02.01.04 Other
        2.02.02 Fire
                2.02.02.01 Evacuation
                2.02.02.02 Firefighting equipment
        2.02.03 Injury
                2.02.03.01 First aid
                2.02.03.02 Other
        2.02.04 Broken equipment
                2.02.04.01 Appliances
                2.02.04.02 Tools
                2.02.04.03 Other
        2.02.05 Structural damage

H/II H: The Learner Will Maintain Foodstock

One problem with which learners must come to grips is that of maintaining foodstocks. Periodically, the stock of food must be inventoried and new foods purchased. This act is complicated because different foods tend to be depleted on different schedules (sometimes approaching randomness). Raisins, for example, must be replaced on a completely different schedule than meat, and bread and milk usually run out more often than rice does. The fact that the task is complicated means only that it requires very careful instruction.

1. Inventory foodstock
   1.01 Pantry
   1.02 Refrigerator
   1.03 Other storage areas

2. Purchase food as required
   2.01 Appropriate quantity
   2.02 Appropriate quality

3. Store food
   3.01 Appropriate locations
   3.02 Appropriate containers
   3.03 Appropriate procedures

H/II I: The Learner Will Prepare and Serve Meals

Preparing and serving meals is also very complicated. Menus must be balanced, and the quantity must be sufficient but not overly so. In addition, food preparation per se requires one to use complicated timing procedures so that all of the food is ready simultaneously.

1. Prepare menus
   1.01 Nutritional balance
   1.02 Variety
   1.03 Appropriate quantity
   1.04 Other

2. Prepare meals
   2.01 Appropriate quantities
   2.02 Appropriate timing
   2.03 Appetizing appearance

3. Serve meals
   3.01 Set table
   3.02 Serve
   3.03 Clean up

4. Preserve and store leftovers
   4.01 Dry foods
   4.02 Liquids
   4.03 Other

5. Other

H/II J: The Learner Will Budget Money Appropriately

Budgeting underlies independent living for anyone. It is most critical for those with limited incomes (as is the case for many low-functioning persons). Even learners with no major income limitations must decide what must/can be done with whatever income is available and allocate actual funds to the places they must go.

1. Obtain income on schedule(s)

2. Cash check(s)

3. Use bank services
   3.01 Savings account
   3.02 Checking account
   3.03 Other

4. Allocate funds appropriately
   4.01 Rent
   4.02 Utilities
       4.02.01 Heat
       4.02.02 Electricity
       4.02.03 Telephone
       4.02.04 Other
   4.03 Food
       4.03.01 Market
       4.03.02 Restaurant
   4.04 Transportation
   4.05 Personal care
       4.05.01 Supplies
       4.05.02 Equipment
       4.05.03 Services
               4.05.03.01 Barber/beauty shop
               4.05.03.02 Laundry
               4.05.03.03 Other
   4.06 Clothing
   4.07 Supplies
   4.08 Equipment

    4.09 Taxes
        4.09.01 Income (state and federal)
        4.09.02 Excise
        4.09.03 Sales
        4.09.04 Other
    4.10 Savings
    4.11 Recreation
    4.12 Emergency expenses
    4.13 Other

H/II K: The Learner Will Pay Bills

Budgeting and allocating funds starts the process, but then the learner must actually pay the bills. The fixed and required expenses must be paid first; any money left over can be used for recreational purposes.

1. Pay fixed bills
    1.01 Food
    1.02 Rent
    1.03 Utilities
    1.04 Transportation
    1.05 Taxes
    1.06 Required repairs
    1.07 Required maintenance
    1.08 Other

2. Purchase necessities
    2.01 Food
    2.02 Equipment
        2.02.01 Cleaning materials
        2.02.02 Other
    2.03 Clothing
    2.04 Equipment
    2.05 Personal needs
    2.06 Other

3. Deposit savings

4. Pay for recreation

5. Other

H/III: GOALS RELATED TO COEXISTING IN A NEIGHBORHOOD AND COMMUNITY

Independent living requires each person to be able to get along with other people. Many learners will never become social butterflies, but they must at least get along with the neighbors, the local merchants and service personnel, and the local constabulary. "Getting along" includes not only saying and doing things that are required, but also *not* saying or doing certain things. It also includes protecting oneself from harm and keeping out of trouble.

H/III A: The Learner Will Interact Appropriately With Others in the Community

Appropriate interactions are a necessity for anyone who intends to live as part of a community. Each and every one of us interacts daily with neighbors, merchants, service personnel, and others, and our interactions must be well within bounds or we will attract negative attention. When we go to stores, we do and say the things that people do and say in stores; when we talk to the neighbors, we do and say the things that neighbors do and say. In addition to actively doing things, however, it is also necessary to *refrain* from doing certain things, such as engaging the next–door neighbor in a long conversation about the weather when that neighbor has a yard full of company.

1. Perform required interactions
    1.01 Neighbors
        1.01.01 Next–door neighbors
        1.01.02 Close neighbors
        1.01.03 Nearby community residents
    1.02 Merchants
        1.02.01 Stores
        1.02.02 Itinerant
        1.02.03 Other

    1.03 Service personnel
        1.03.01 Repair
        1.03.02 Delivery
        1.03.03 Meter readers
        1.03.04 Other
    1.04 Officials
        1.04.01 Law enforcement
        1.04.02 Welfare officials
        1.04.03 Other

2. Refrain from interacting inappropriately

3. Observe demeanor constraints
    3.01 Deference
    3.02 Assertiveness
    3.03 Familiarity
    3.04 Other

4. Observe conversational constraints
    4.01 Topics
    4.02 Length
    4.03 Other

5. Exhibit appropriate body language
    5.01 Posture
    5.02 Facial expressions
    5.03 Gestures
    5.04 Movements
    5.05 Other

H/III B: The Learner Will Respond Appropriately to the Inappropriate Conduct of Others in the Community

It will sometimes happen that another person or persons in the community will attempt to harass or victimize the learner. Learners must be prepared to respond if this happens. If the inappropriate behavior continues, life can become intolerable.

1. Identify inappropriate conduct of others
    1.01 Aggression
        1.01.01 Physical
        1.01.02 Verbal
        1.01.03 Other
    1.02 Manipulation
        1.02.01 Legal
        1.02.02 Financial
        1.02.03 Social
        1.02.04 Other
    1.03 Harassment
        1.03.01 Physical
        1.03.02 Verbal
        1.03.03 Sexual
        1.03.04 Other
    1.04 Cheating
    1.05 Other

2. Respond to inappropriate conduct of others
    2.01 Avoid contact
    2.02 Seek assistance
        2.02.01 Law enforcement
        2.02.02 Legal
        2.02.03 Financial
        2.02.04 Friends/neighbors
        2.02.05 Other
    2.03 Other

H/III C: The Learner Will Observe the Requirements of the Law

In order to continue to live in the community, everyone must try to stay out of trouble with the law. In part, this requirement involves doing things, such as observing moderation in the public consumption of alcohol. In part, it also involves *not* doing things, such as stealing. In addition, every member of the community has certain rights (e.g., if arrested, or if "down" financially). These rights may have to be exercised and learners should know how to do this.

1. Refrain from illegal acts
    1.01 Stealing
    1.02 Public drunkenness
    1.03 Sexual acts
    1.04 Vehicle usage
    1.05 Disturbing the peace
    1.06 Other

2. Actively observe the requirements of the law
    2.01 Traffic laws
        2.01.01 Pedestrian
        2.01.02 Vehicle
    2.02 Nuisance laws
        2.02.01 Noise
        2.02.02 Alcohol
        2.02.03 Loitering
        2.02.04 Other
    2.03 Use of public facilities
        2.03.01 Public restrooms
        2.03.02 Public parks
        2.03.03 Public streets
        2.03.04 Public buildings
        2.03.05 Other
    2.04 Property
    2.05 Contract
    2.06 Other

3. Exercise rights if arrested
    3.01 Telephone calls
    3.02 Representation
    3.03 Other

H/III D: The Learner Will Carry Out Civic Responsibilities

Like everyone else, low-functioning persons have a right to help others in the community. In addition, like everyone else, they must obey the law—that is, do such things as register for the draft and jury duty.

1. Register for duties
    1.01 Draft
    1.02 Voting
    1.03 Other

2. Carry out responsibilities
    2.01 Attend civic meetings
    2.02 Vote
    2.03 Fulfill jury duty
    2.04 Other

3. Volunteer for community service
    3.01 Public service
    3.02 Political work
    3.03 Charity work
    3.04 Other

H/IV: GOALS RELATED TO THE
HANDLING OF GLITCHES

Many low-functioning persons find it difficult to deal with problems, but they are everywhere; nobody goes through a nice, smooth day. We all have had the experience of getting up in the morning only to find that we forgot to buy toothpaste, or that the electricity went out last night and the alarm clock did not go off on time. Later in the day we may burn the steak or break the salt shaker. Murphy's Law is always potentially in force. Living in a community and neighborhood has its own special set of problems with which everyone must deal.

H/IV A: The Learner Will Cope With Equipment Breakdowns

Machines invariably break down, normally when we try to use them to do something. It is necessary to teach low-functioning persons how to handle such breakdowns and not to be "thrown" by them.

1. Identify broken equipment
   1.01 Housecleaning equipment
   1.02 Clothing maintenance equipment
   1.03 Food preparation equipment
   1.04 Maintenance/repair equipment
   1.05 Other

2. Respond appropriately to broken equipment
   2.01 Postpone tasks
   2.02 Repair equipment
      2.02.01 Self
      2.02.02 Equipment repair business
   2.03 Discard nonrepairable equipment
   2.04 Replace discarded equipment

H/IV B: The Learner Will Cope With Household Supplies Depletion

Supplies are used up and their depletion is sometimes unanticipated. Generally, such depletion is discovered at inconvenient times. Again, learners must be taught how to handle such problems.

1. Identify depleted materials
    1.01 Housecleaning materials
    1.02 Home maintenance materials
    1.03 Clothing maintenance materials
    1.04 Other
2. Respond appropriately to depleted materials
    2.01 Postpone task performance
    2.02 Replace materials
        2.02.01 Borrow temporary supply
        2.02.02 Make trip to store
    2.03 Change task performance
    2.04 Perform alternate task

H/IV C: The Learner Will Cope With Unexpected Depletions of Funds

Events often occur that cause people suddenly to be without funds, for example, money gets lost or stolen, unexpected expenses deplete available funds, etc. When it happens, normal expenditures may have to be postponed and it is sometimes necessary to develop a method to handle the problem.

1. Identify sudden depletion of funds
   1.01 Unexpected expenditures
       1.01.01 Emergency
       1.01.02 Unwise decisions
       1.01.03 Actions of others
       1.01.04 Other
   1.02 Overdrawn account
   1.03 Theft
   1.04 Loss of money
   1.05 Other

2. Respond appropriately to fund depletion
   2.01 Rebudget
   2.02 Borrow
       2.02.01 Family/friends
       2.02.02 Loan agency
       2.02.03 Other

H/IV D: The Learner Will Respond Appropriately to Disruptions of Routines

Probably the most common glitch of all is disruption of the daily routine. Sometimes things just never seem to happen when they are supposed to. Despite the fact that things and events interrupt the routine, it is necessary to get done what has to get done.

1. Identify disruption of routine
    1.01 Company
    1.02 Holidays
    1.03 Early completion of chores
    1.04 Other

2. Cope with disruption of routine
    2.01 Postpone task performance
    2.02 Perform alternate tasks
    2.03 Other

H/IV E: The Learner Will Respond Appropriately to Sudden Changes in the Weather

No matter how we prepare for seasonal changes, the unexpected always seems to occur. Storms blow up and the windows must be closed, and in the autumn the weather gets cold and then suddenly turns warm again (the opposite occurs in the spring). Such glitches require one to be ready for change, especially at certain times of the year.

1. Observe sudden weather changes
    1.01 Rainstorms
    1.02 Heat/cold fronts
    1.03 Wind
    1.04 Other

2. Respond to required changes in heating
    2.01 Increase
    2.02 Decrease

3. Respond to required changes in building structure
    3.01 Storm doors and windows
    3.02 Screens
    3.03 Other

4. Respond to required changes in clothing

Chapter 7

Domain V
Vocational

People who are independent work. Their jobs may or may not be well paid, and they may or may not have prestige. Whatever the case, independent people work. In fact, if a person does not hold a recognized job (which may include working at home, e.g., on the family farm or keeping house), it may prove impossible for that person to establish and maintain control over his or her own life. Therefore, like everyone else, low-functioning persons should have jobs. But holding a job is complicated. For example, it is necessary to find work before doing it. And once one gets a job, it is necessary to maintain employment, a task that involves more than simply doing the job. With the exception of women (and now some men) who choose to work at home, most jobs are located someplace other than where we live. Consequently, most workers are required to follow time schedules no matter how far away they live or how difficult it is to get to work. They must do their jobs, respond to many problems by themselves, and get along with others, such as the boss and fellow workers. And, as is true in all the domains, the daily glitches must be handled. Complicated though it may be, all the above and more is required to maintain one's position in the workplace.

V/I: GOALS AND OBJECTIVES
RELATED TO OBTAINING WORK

To develop and maintain control over one's life, it is necessary to seek work from time to time. While it is entirely possible that the learner's first job will also be the only job he ever needs, it is probable that he will have to seek other employment several times during his lifespan. Therefore, one focus of instruction should be on "how to do it."

V/I A: The Learner Will Seek Employment

Obtaining work is a complicated matter. Even when jobs are plentiful, not every available job is suitable for everyone. We all have likes and dislikes, strengths and weaknesses, and various jobs suit different people differently. In addition, factors such as the physical locations of jobs, pay levels, and desirability of the work environments all figure into the choice of whether to work in one place or another (assuming that the job search has made more than one job available). Therefore, it is necessary not only to teach learners how to seek work, but to teach them how to choose from among different jobs.

1. Search for employment
   1.01 Use formal networks
      1.01.01 Want ads
      1.01.02 Employment services
      1.01.03 Other
   1.02 Use informal networks
      1.02.01 Relatives
      1.02.02 Friends
      1.02.03 Other

2. Apply for employment
   2.01 Obtain and complete application
   2.02 Interview for jobs
   2.03 Other

3. Assess job desirability
   3.01 Assess job requirements
      3.01.01 Motor skill requirements
      3.01.02 Strength requirements
      3.01.03 Academic skill requirements
      3.01.04 Problem-solving skill requirements
      3.01.05 Endurance requirements
      3.01.06 Other
   3.02 Assess work environment
      3.02.01 Safety features
      3.02.02 Health features
      3.02.03 Employee facilities
      3.02.04 Barriers
      3.02.05 Work climate
      3.02.06 Other

3.03 Assess compensation
    3.03.01 Salary
    3.03.02 Benefits
    3.03.03 Other
3.04 Assess location of work
    3.04.01 Availability of transportation
    3.04.02 Travel distance
    3.04.03 Travel time
    3.04.04 Potential danger, e.g., in neighborhood
    3.04.05 Other

V/I B: The Learner Will Accept Employment

The learner who has decided to accept a job offer must indicate to the employer that he agrees to do the job. In addition, it is necessary to perform certain other pre-job tasks, such as filling out tax deduction forms.

1. Indicate acceptance of the job

2. Fill out W-4 form

3. Submit to physical exam

4. Other

V/I C: The Learner Will Utilize Unemployment Services

At one time or another, many persons experience unemployment: they quit, get laid off, get fired, or their jobs simply disappear for one reason or another. If it happens, it is necessary to know how to use the services that are available in the community while seeking employment.

1. Apply for unemployment benefits

2. Request job search assistance
    2.01 Employment Security Division
    2.02 Vocational rehabilitation agency
    2.03 Other local agency

V/II: GOALS AND OBJECTIVES
RELATED TO
PERFORMING THE WORK
ROUTINE

A major requirement for everyone who works is to perform the job for which they were hired. The work routine includes doing the assigned work as well as maintaining the workstation. In addition, some workers may be expected to do things such as fill in for others who are absent. Performing the work routine also requires a worker to deal directly or indirectly with several different time concepts (even when they cannot state them): *Point* ("now," "yesterday," "3 o'clock," "two weeks from tomorrow," etc.); *Duration* ("20 minutes," "all day," "the weekend," etc.); and *Rate* ("20 mph," "three per day," etc.). These concepts are involved in matters such as regular attendance and meeting work performance standards.

V/II A: The Learner Will Perform the Job Routine

Workers must do their jobs, but maintaining employment can include tasks other than the one for which the worker was hired. For example, especially in small businesses, workers are sometimes required to fill in for others who may be absent. They must also exhibit the correct use of facilities provided for employees, such as cafeterias and toilets.

1. Learn to do the work
    1.01 Required tasks
    1.02 Sequence of tasks
    1.03 Clothing changes
        1.03.01 Dirty clothing
        1.03.02 Uniforms
        1.03.03 Protective equipment
        1.03.04 Other

2. Learn to perform other work that may occasionally be required
    2.01 Required tasks
    2.02 Fill ins
    2.03 Other

3. Handle early completion of assigned tasks
    3.01 New task identification
    3.02 New task performance

4. Learn the location of facilities
    4.01 Lunchroom
    4.02 Restrooms
    4.03 Lounge
    4.04 Other

5. Perform the job routine

6. Observe acceptable limits of local work production rate

7. Observe local work quality standards

V/II B: The Learner Will Follow Work-Related Daily Schedule

Workers who can perform a job very well may lose it because of some nontask factor as habitual tardiness. Therefore, it is just as necessary to teach learners to respond to the nonwork parameters of the job, such as those relating to time as to the work itself.

1. Follow daily work schedule
    1.01 Regular attendance
    1.02 Starting/quitting times
    1.03 Rest and lunch breaks
    1.04 Split shifts
    1.05 Other

2. Follow nonwork schedule
    2.01 Days off
    2.02 Holidays
    2.03 Vacations
    2.04 Other

V/II C: The Learner Will Maintain the Workstation

Jobs have varying degrees of clutter and dirt associated with them. Maintaining the workstation means one thing to a trash collector (gas the vehicle, put air in the tires, hose out the bin), and quite another to a janitor (store cleaning tools and materials, arrange furniture). Workers usually must maintain their workstations as part of the job.

1. Observe environmental maintenance standards
    1.01 Cleanliness
    1.02 Clutter

2. Follow environmental maintenance schedules
    2.01 Cleanliness
    2.02 Clutter

3. Use maintenance tools/materials

4. Replenish/replace/maintain maintenance tools/materials as needed

5. Store job/maintenance tools and materials

6. Store clean/dirty clothing

V/II D: The Learner Will Follow Employer Rules and Regulations

Every employer has a set of rules and regulations, which may be expressed verbally or in writing. These rules generally focus on things the employer has found to be problematical, such as attendance problems, stealing, and drinking on the job, along with a host of other possibilities. In addition, there may be other unexpressed (but real) rules. Because an employee may be discharged for breaking any of these rules, they must be learned and followed.

1. Learn employer rules and regulations
   1.01 Attendance
   1.02 Controlled substances
   1.03 Stealing
   1.04 Chain of command
   1.05 Paid/unpaid leave
   1.06 Reporting absences
   1.07 Reporting problems
   1.08 Other

2. Follow employer rules

V/II E: The Learner Will Use Facilities Appropriately

Most employers have rules governing the use of facilities. For example, there may be schedules for their use or workers may be required to obtain permission prior to leaving the job station to use a facility. Workers who do not follow these rules or patterns will soon attract attention.

1. Follow established usage patterns of facilities
   1.01 Breaks
   1.02 Lunch
   1.03 Other

2. Follow standard behavior patterns in facilities

3. Obtain facility usage permissions as necessary

V/II F: The Learner Will Follow Safety Procedures While on the Job

Each job has its own set of safety procedures workers must learn to perform. The most common of these involve the use of safety equipment and clothing, equipment and materials, storage, and neatness. There may be others as well, such as behavior relative to nearby equipment or other workers.

1. Use tools and materials appropriately

2. Store tools and materials

3. Perform job activities

4. Keep job station free of safety hazards
   4.01 Cleanliness and clutter
   4.02 Nearby equipment

5. Use safety equipment
   5.01 Clothing
   5.02 Eye/ear protection
   5.03 Head protection
   5.04 Shoes
   5.05 Other

6. Refrain from entering unsafe areas

7. Follow supervisor's directions in unusual circumstances

V/II G: The Learner Will Follow Accident and Emergency Procedures

Accidents happen despite everyone's best efforts to prevent them. Because there is no such thing as an accident/emergency free environment, every workplace has (or should have) accident and emergency procedures. It is vital for all workers to understand these procedures and to follow them when necessary.

1. Follow standard accident/emergency reporting procedures

2. Follow standard accident/emergency action procedures

3. Follow standard first aid procedures

V/III: GOALS RELATED TO
COEXISTING WITH OTHERS ON
THE JOB

Each job requires workers to interact with others: supervisor(s), fellow workers, perhaps the public, and sometimes even subordinates (low-functioning persons have indeed become supervisors). Interactions with all of these people are of the utmost importance in maintaining employment; saying or doing the wrong thing can result in loss of a job. Consequently, interpersonal interactions at work constitute a major area of instruction for low-functioning persons.

V/III A: The Learner Will Interact Appropriately With Others on the Job

Doing and saying the appropriate things while on the job will allow a worker to be seen by other workers as "belonging." Each job has its own interactions and required noninteractions, all of which must be observed. It would be inappropriate, for example, to distract one's supervisor with extended conversation about last week's cut finger or to attempt to interact with the customers of a business if one is not supposed to come in contact with the public. In addition, each job allows certain types of conversations and certain kinds of demeanor. If learners are to be seen as successful employees, they must learn how to do these things.

1. Perform required interactions
   1.01 Supervisor
   1.02 Fellow workers
   1.03 Public
   1.04 Subordinates
   1.05 Other

2. Refrain from inappropriate interactions

3. Observe demeanor constraints
   3.01 Deference
   3.02 Assertiveness
   3.03 Familiarity
   3.04 Other

4. Observe conversational constraints
   4.01 Topics
   4.02 Length
   4.03 Other

5. Exhibit appropriate body language
   5.01 Posture
   5.02 Facial expressions
   5.03 Gestures
   5.04 Movements
   5.05 Other

V/III B: The Learner Will Respond Appropriately to the Inappropriate Conduct of Others on the Job

Every job has its social problems. Sometimes fellow workers will "pick on" another worker for the sport of it, and sometimes personality conflicts will cause a supervisor or fellow worker to behave with enmity toward the learner. In addition, jobs that involve contact with the public require workers to cope with the rudeness of some of the people with whom they must come in contact. All of these problems must be dealt with appropriately if the worker is to last on the job.

1. Identify the inappropriate conduct of others
   1.01 Aggression
      1.01.01 Physical
      1.01.02 Verbal
      1.01.03 Other
   1.02 Manipulation
      1.02.01 Setups
      1.02.02 Production
      1.02.03 Excessive demands
      1.02.04 Other
   1.03 Rudeness
   1.04 Lollygagging
   1.05 Insubordination
   1.06 Harassment
      1.06.01 Physical
      1.06.02 Verbal
      1.06.03 Sexual
      1.06.04 Other
   1.07 Other

2. Respond to the inappropriate conduct of others
   2.01 Follow company procedures
   2.02 Obtain assistance
      2.02.01 Friends
      2.02.02 Family
      2.02.03 Officials
      2.02.04 Other
   2.03 Other

3. Avoid contact with troublemakers

4. Other

V/IV: GOALS RELATED TO
HANDLING GLITCHES

Like everyone else, a low-functioning person's day will have its glitches: the bus is late and so is the worker, somebody did not come into work today and the boss needs someone to fill in at another workstation, materials run out too soon, etc., etc. Anything can and will go wrong. In setting up a curriculum, it is necessary to be mindful of such glitches and to train learners to handle them prior to the time they go off on their own.

V/IV A: The Learner Will Cope With Changes in Work Routine

Workers can expect to experience variations in work routines, such as filling in for other workers who may be absent or engaged in other tasks or accommodating sudden changes in work emphasis generated by business surges or cutbacks, etc. Events such as these may place workers in the position of having to make unexpected changes in work patterns, and they must be ready to handle them. In addition, every job has its downtime. Many jobs require the worker to "look busy," while others require the worker to do different tasks. The learner must follow whatever procedures are required.

Workers can have other changes in work schedules. Overtime, rotating shifts, layoffs, and other events all cause the worker to have to readjust his timeframe and to work more or fewer hours in a given week than would ordinarily be the case. Learners must be prepared for such changes in schedule.

1. Follow required work routine changes

2. Follow emergency/nonemergency attendance procedures
   2.01 Telephone calls
   2.02 Documentation
   2.03 Other

3. Follow procedures for unexpected downtime

4. Make required schedule changes

V/IV B: The Learner Will Cope With Work Problems

Every job has its troubles—equipment breaks down, materials run out, etc. These problems are not caused by accident or emergency and do not pose physical threats to anyone. But they do bring work to a halt, and employees must respond to them appropriately. Some problems must be reported to supervisors, while others should be handled by the employee without reporting them to the supervisor. Workers must know not only which work problems to report, but also which not to report.

1. Identify problems
   1.01 Reportable/nonreportable
   1.02 Employee/supervisor responsibility

2. Respond to problem
   2.01 Employee–handled
   2.02 Supervisor–handled

V/IV C: The Learner Will Cope With Work Supply Depletions and Equipment Breakdowns

Workers often must deal with the fact that supplies run out unexpectedly, or that equipment stops working. Janitors run out of cleaning fluid, machines run out of gasoline, and electric motors short out. When such things happen, workers must be able to do something to keep the work flow moving, if possible, or to obtain assistance where necessary.

1. Identify supply depletion or equipment breakdown
    1.01 Tools
    1.02 Materials
2. Respond appropriately to supply depletion or equipment breakdown
    2.01 Follow required procedures
        2.01.01 Notify responsible person
        2.01.02 Wait for assistance
    2.02 Take appropriate action
        2.02.01 Replenish supply
        2.02.02 Replace material
        2.02.03 Repair equipment
        2.02.04 Replace equipment
        2.02.05 Other

Chapter 8
Domain L
Leisure

For independent persons, leisure should be a time of renewal, a break from the required activities of daily life. After working hard all day, coming home and cooking a meal, cleaning up the mess, and perhaps completing another chore or two, one really should be able to do something one would *like* to do. Leisure is an accepted part of our industrialized society, and low-functioning people should be able to participate as fully in leisure activities as possible, just as in any other facet of life. It is necessary to be mindful of the fact, however, that the one concept discriminating the Leisure Domain from the others is choice: the person who engages in a leisure activity chooses to do so; otherwise it could not be a true leisure activity. This fact makes instruction in the Leisure Domain more difficult than instruction in the other domains because it is more difficult to plan the required instructional programs. The dilemma: if we try to teach a leisure skill to a learner, and if the learner does not want to perform that leisure skill, then we are not teaching leisure skills. It is an interesting and challenging problem, and one to which there is no easy response.

L/I: GOALS RELATED TO
DEVELOPING LEISURE
ACTIVITIES

People who engage in activities may seek out the company of others or they may do things alone; they may engage in organized activities, or they may do things haphazardly; they may engage in active pursuits or they may engage in passive pursuits. Their leisure activities may range from participation in organized competitive sports to flopping down in front of the television, and from solitary walks through natural settings to theatergoing in large crowds. Whatever the activity, one must learn how to do it at some time before doing much of it.

L/I A: The Learner Will Find Appropriate New Leisure Activities

Everyone develops new friends and interests and otherwise evolves different leisure activities during the course of life. Consequently, most people change their preferred leisure activities from time to time. Some activities continue across the years; for example, family gatherings, television viewing, etc., are common, ongoing leisure activities for many people. But most people tire of unrelieved television viewing, and activities on the order of family gatherings tend to occur occasionally rather than constantly. Therefore, to become independent, low-functioning persons, like everyone else, must develop new leisure activities from time to time. To do so, it is necessary first to discover what activities exist. Then, factors such as the cost of the activities will have to be weighed against the availability of funds and the desirability of the activity. If everything works out, the learner can begin learning how to perform the activity.

1. Identify potential leisure activity
    1.01 Use formal networks
        1.01.01 Advertisements
        1.01.02 Leisure activity agencies
        1.01.03 Other
    1.02 Use informal networks
        1.02.01 Family
        1.02.02 Friends/acquaintances
        1.02.03 Other

2. Assess desirability of potential leisure activity
 2.01 Projected benefits
  2.01.01 Social
  2.01.02 Physical
  2.01.03 Entertainment value
  2.01.04 Other
 2.02 Personal abilities/disabilities
  2.02.01 Physical
  2.02.02 Intellectual
  2.02.03 Other
 2.03 Accessibility
  2.03.01 Location
  2.03.02 Distance
  2.03.03 Available transportation
  2.03.04 Time required for travel
 2.04 Facilities

3. Assess ability to pay required costs
 3.01 Cost
  3.01.01 Fees
  3.01.02 Required equipment
  3.01.03 Other
 3.02 Available income
  3.02.01 Fixed expenses
  3.02.02 Funds available for leisure

L/I B: The Learner Will Acquire Skills Required for Leisure Activities

Once one decides to engage in a specific leisure activity, it is necessary to learn how to do it. Some leisure activities require only minimal skills, such as going to the local park to listen to band concerts. In such a case, the only learning involved may be that of finding out how to get out of the house on time. On the other hand, sometimes great dedication is required to develop skills, as for athletic competition or music. In these cases, it may be necessary to take lessons for an extended period of time.

1. Acquire skills through formal lessons
   1.01 Classes
   1.02 Individual instruction
   1.03 Other

2. Acquire skills informally
   2.01 Observation
   2.02 Informal instruction
        2.02.01 Friends/acquaintances
        2.02.02 Existing participants
   2.03 Printed materials
   2.04 Trial and error
   2.05 Other

L/II: GOALS RELATED TO PERFORMING LEISURE ACTIVITY ROUTINES

Once acquisition of skills begins, the learner may want to perform the leisure activity. It will be performed in the context of a routine much like those for work and maintaining the living quarters. Establishing and performing the leisure routine is as much a part of the activity as is learning the skills per se. In addition, facilities in which leisure activities are performed often have rules governing both their use and the behavioral patterns users are expected to exhibit; for example, athletic facilities have schedules and patterns that all users are expected to follow, and the learner who goes to a movie and stands up in front of the other patrons during the film will be asked to leave the theater. Whatever the rules, the learner must follow them or he or she will not be allowed to participate.

L/II A: The Learner Will Perform Leisure Activities

1. Establish activity schedule
   1.01 Select activities
   1.02 Schedule available time
       1.02.01 Personal off hours
       1.02.02 Working hours
       1.02.03 Required homemaking chores
       1.02.04 Required personal maintenance chores
       1.02.05 Other required activities
       1.02.06 Available facility time
       1.02.07 Available time of fellow participants
       1.02.08 Other

2. Prepare activity peripherals
   2.01 Clothing
   2.02 Equipment
   2.03 Money
   2.04 Other

3. Engage in activities
   3.01 Pay required fees
   3.02 Use clothing/equipment
   3.03 Obtain required equipment
   3.04 Follow rules of activity
   3.05 Other

4. Follow usage patterns
   4.01 Starting and ending time(s)
   4.02 Permissions
   4.03 Equipment rental
   4.04 Appropriate activity patterns

5. Other

L/II B: The Learner Will Maintain Personal Leisure Equipment

If the learner's leisure activities require the use of equipment, it usually must be maintained. Tools and equipment require lubrication, adjustment, repair, cleaning, storing, etc. If equipment is not maintained, the learner may find himself unable to perform the activity.

1. Replenish depleted supplies as needed

2. Replace worn or defective equipment and materials as needed

3. Make necessary repairs and adjustments to equipment

4. Store leisure equipment during off times
   4.01 Space
   4.02 Racks, holders, hangers, etc.
   4.03 Storage techniques
        4.03.01 Seasonal equipment
        4.03.02 Regularly used equipment
   4.04 Other

5. Clean clothing and equipment as required

L/II C: The Learner Will Follow Leisure Safety Procedures

Some leisure activities are more hazardous than others: motorcycle riding, skydiving, and surfing are all very hazardous, while TV viewing, strolling in the park, and chatting over the back fence with neighbors are relatively safe. Nevertheless, even the latter group of activities can have its dangers. Electrical storms, for example, can make strolling in the park an extremely dangerous activity. The learners must learn not only how and when to perform the activity, but also how to do it safely. In addition, many activities require attention to the environment, for instance, not leaving things lying around that might cause someone to be hurt, or not engaging in the activity until all persons are in safe locations.

1. Follow all safety rules for leisure activity

2. Follow all safety rules for leisure facility use

3. Use equipment appropriately

4. Store equipment

5. Keep leisure location and equipment free of hazards
    5.01 Cleanliness and clutter
    5.02 Needed repairs
    5.03 Required discards
        5.03.01 Broken equipment
        5.03.02 Equipment worn beyond use
    5.04 Other

6. Use safety equipment
    6.01 Body protection for self
    6.02 Equipment for safety of others
    6.03 Other

7. Refrain from entering unsafe areas

8. Follow directions of officials relative to safety

9. Observe moderation in the use of alcohol and other substances during performance of activities

L/II D: The Learner Will Follow Accident and Emergency Procedures for Leisure Activities

Emergencies lurk around every corner: the learner or one of his fellow activity participants may be injured, or become ill; sudden telephone calls from home may indicate trouble to which the learner must respond; a storm may do damage to the facility in which the activity is taking place, etc. Whatever happens, the learner must respond appropriately to emergencies.

1. Identify accident/emergency
   1.01 Injury/illness
      1.01.01 Self
      1.01.02 Other
   1.02 Other

2. Follow standard accident/emergency reporting procedures
   2.01 Inform responsible person nearby
   2.02 Local emergency telephone number
   2.03 Police/fire telephone
   2.04 Other

3. Follow standard accident/emergency action procedures
   3.01 Directions from responsible person
   3.02 Standard first aid procedures

4. Cancel or postpone activity

5. Other

L/III: GOALS RELATED TO
COEXISTING WITH OTHERS
DURING LEISURE TIMES

As is true in each of the other domains, leisure involves interactions with other people. The interactions are both those that must be performed, and those that must *not* be performed. It is interesting to note that leisure activities may be performed with others or alone, and that in either instance the learner may find himself in the company of others or may be totally removed from others. For example, one can go to the movies alone, but the theater may be full of people. On the other end of the scale, a group of people may go to a deserted location for a private group picnic. Even when one is alone in the living quarters watching television, it is necessary to be aware that other people may be involved, such as when the sound is so loud that it bothers the neighbors. Those who do not exhibit appropriate behavior patterns will attract negative attention.

L/III A: The Learner Will Interact Appropriately With Others During Leisure Activities

During leisure activities many interactions are required. Whatever the interactions (or required noninteractions), there are usually rules to follow. Team activities, for example, require one to interact with both fellow team members and members of the opposing team—two very different kinds of interaction. In addition, there are always officials of some sort, and there may be bystanders or observers. All must be responded to appropriately.

1. Perform required interactions
   1.01 Officials
       1.01.01 Money takers
       1.01.02 Activity directors
       1.01.03 Rule enforcers
       1.01.04 Other
   1.02 Fellow participants
       1.02.01 Cooperating participants
           1.02.01.01 Same team
           1.02.01.02 Opponents
       1.02.02 Parallel participants
       1.02.03 Other

    1.03 Observers
        1.03.01 Audience
        1.03.02 Bystanders
    1.04 Other

2. Refrain from inappropriate interactions

3. Observe demeanor constraints
    3.01 Deference
    3.02 Assertiveness
    3.03 Familiarity
    3.04 Other

4. Observe conversational constraints
    4.01 Topics
    4.02 Length
    4.03 Other

5. Exhibit appropriate body language
    5.01 Posture
    5.02 Facial expressions
    5.03 Gestures
    5.04 Movements
    5.05 Other

L/III B: The Learner Will Respond Appropriately to the Inappropriate Conduct of Others During Leisure Activity

Even during leisure activities when one is supposed to be enjoying oneself, conflict with others can and does arise. To some extent it must be handled differently than conflict at work or in the neighborhood. For one thing, the effects of avoiding contact with the person(s) with whom one is in conflict are different during leisure than they are during work activities. For another, contact with others at work or in the neighborhood may be unavoidable, but because leisure activities depend so heavily on choice, contact with conflicting others may be more easily avoided.

1. Identify the inappropriate conduct of others
    1.01 Aggression
        1.01.01 Physical
        1.01.02 Verbal
        1.01.03 Other
    1.02 Rudeness
    1.03 Harassment
        1.03.01 Physical
        1.03.02 Verbal
        1.03.03 Sexual
        1.03.04 Other
    1.04 Teasing
    1.05 Breaking facility behavioral patterns
    1.06 Other

2. Respond to the inappropriate conduct of others
    2.01 Follow facility procedures
        2.01.01 Reporting
        2.01.02 Other
    2.02 Obtain assistance
        2.02.01 Friends
        2.02.02 Officials
        2.02.03 Other
    2.03 Avoid contact with troublemakers
    2.04 Other

L/IV: GOALS RELATED TO
HANDLING GLITCHES

During leisure, as in all other domains, things can and do go wrong. Rain falls on picnics, facilities close unexpectedly, equipment breaks, materials run out just when one gets ready to use them, etc. The learner must be prepared to cope with such problems.

L/IV A: The Learner Will Respond to Changes in Leisure Routine

Many things can cause a change in the leisure routine: weather can ruin an outing, fellow participants may get sick or have to respond to an emergency, the learner himself may have to do something else, etc. Whatever happens, the learner must develop ways in which to deal with the problem.

1. Observe schedule changes
   1.01 Weather related
   1.02 Illness related
       1.02.01 Self
       1.02.02 Fellow participants
       1.02.03 Officials
   1.03 Work related
       1.03.01 Overtime
       1.03.02 Shift changes
       1.03.03 Other
   1.04 Other

2. Adapt to schedule changes
   2.01 Reschedule activity
   2.02 Cancel activity
   2.03 Perform alternate activity
   2.04 Other

L/IV B: The Learner Will Cope With Equipment Breakdowns and Materials Depletions

Equipment used in leisure activities can break down and materials can run out. If the learner does not have alternate equipment or materials on hand, or if he has neglected to perform his inventory and obtain replacements ahead of time, it will be necessary to do something.

1. Observe problem
    1.01 Equipment breakdown
        1.01.01 Warranties
        1.01.02 Repairs
    1.02 Materials depletion
    1.03 Other

2. Adapt to problem
    2.01 Repair equipment
    2.02 Replace materials
    2.03 Reschedule activity
        2.03.01 Cancel
        2.03.02 Reschedule
        2.03.03 Alternate activity

Chapter 9

Domain T
Travel

Independence is partly a matter of moving about the community unassisted. Travel skills are necessary in order to go to work, obtain food and supplies, pay bills, go to church, and develop an array of leisure and entertainment opportunities, among other things. To travel around the community, it is necessary not only to locomote and use the various means of conveyance (such as buses and taxis), but also to develop "mental maps" of the environment: it is just as necessary to know where one is going as it is to have a means of getting there. There are also a number of time concepts that one must know in order to travel. For example, one must be able to figure when to leave the house to get a bus that will get one to the movie in time to see the show. Also, as for each of the other domains, it is necessary to know how to interact with people. Such people run the gamut from fellow pedestrians to ticket agents. Saying or doing the wrong thing to or in front of them will surely attract negative attention and cause a learner great difficulties. Finally, Travel, like each of the other domains, has its glitches: equipment breaks down, schedules change, etc. The learner who has procedures for responding to these problems will be better off than the one who does not.

T/I: GOALS RELATED TO ROUTINE
TRAVEL IN THE COMMUNITY

It can be argued that we find our way from one place to another by developing mental maps of the environment. Whether or not this is a true characterization of how we actually do it, we all must know where we are going, and we must know when we get there. Low-functioning people, like everyone else, must develop such understandings in order to become independent.

T/I A: The Learner Will Develop Mental Maps of Frequented Buildings

Mental maps can be simple or they can be complex. Perhaps the simplest is the understanding of how to get from one place to another within the buildings one frequents.

1. Travel to locations in living quarters
    1.01 Living room(s)
    1.02 Kitchen
    1.03 Bedroom(s)
    1.04 Other

2. Travel to locations in school
    2.01 Homeroom
        2.01.01 Locations in homeroom
        2.01.02 To homeroom from all other locations
    2.02 Bus stop
    2.03 Cafeteria
    2.04 Other frequented rooms
    2.05 Outdoor areas
    2.06 Offices
    2.07 Hall

3. Travel to locations at the job site
   3.01 Workstation
   3.02 Facilities
      3.02.01 Restrooms
      3.02.02 Eating area(s)
      3.02.03 Other
   3.03 Supervisor's station

4. Travel to locations within community sites
   4.01 Mall/shopping center
   4.02 Store sections
      4.02.01 Goods
      4.02.02 Services
      4.02.03 Restrooms
      4.02.04 Other
   4.03 Public building(s)
      4.03.01 Offices
      4.03.02 Restrooms
      4.03.03 Other
   4.04 Other

5. Travel to locations at leisure site(s)
   5.01 Activity site(s)
   5.02 Toilet(s)
   5.03 Washroom(s)
   5.04 Other

T/I B: The Learner Will Develop Mental Maps of the Community

The second major set of mental maps are those that allow us to move about the community with assurance. They allow us not only to go from our living quarters to other locations in the community, but also between locations, such as from one store to another. In other words, mental maps can become very complicated indeed.

1. Travel to stores
    1.01 Grocery store(s)
    1.02 Fast food stores
    1.03 Drug store(s)
    1.04 Discount and department store(s)
    1.05 Shoe store(s)
    1.06 Clothing store(s)
    1.07 Hardware store(s)
    1.08 Shopping centers
    1.09 Other

2. Travel to medical assistance
    2.01 Physician(s)
    2.02 Dentist(s)
    2.03 Chiropractor(s)
    2.04 Hospital
    2.05 Emergency medical treatment
    2.06 Other

3. Travel to restaurants

4. Travel to church

5. Travel to leisure locations
   5.01 Parks
   5.02 Entertainment facilities
      5.02.01 Movies
      5.02.02 Music facilities
      5.02.03 Theaters
      5.02.04 Other
   5.03 Athletic facilities
   5.04 Public gathering spots
   5.05 Other

6. Travel to banks

7. Travel to work site(s)

8. Travel to center city

9. Travel between above locations

T/II: GOALS RELATED
TO THE USE OF CONVEYANCES

Given the emphasis on motorized vehicles in our society, it seems impossible to live without access to transportation in most localities. Perhaps if one lives in a town with a very small population, the need to use conveyances may not arise very often because the distances are small. However, many people live in larger communities and often find it necessary to use conveyances of one type or another. Further, those who work or go to school in communities other than their own are virtually required to use them.

T/II A: The Learner Will Follow Usage Procedures for Conveyances

Any conveyance has usage procedures: riding in a car requires one to shut the doors, buckle the seat belts, etc.; riding a bus requires one to board the bus, pay the fare, find a seat, etc. In order to move independently about the community, low-functioning persons must learn to perform these procedures.

1. Ride in/on private conveyances
   1.01 Bicycle
   1.02 Automobile
   1.03 Van
   1.04 Other

2. Operate private conveyances
   2.01 Operate vehicle
       2.01.01 Bicycle
       2.01.02 Automobile
       2.01.03 Other
   2.02 Observe traffic laws

3. Ride in public conveyances
   3.01 Intracity
       3.01.01 Bus/trolley
       3.01.02 Subway
       3.01.03 Cab
       3.01.04 Other
   3.02 Intercity
       3.02.01 Bus
       3.02.02 Train
       3.02.03 Airplane
       3.02.04 Other
   3.03 Other

T/II B: The Learner Will Make Decisions Preparatory to Travel

Prior to traveling anywhere, the traveler must make certain decisions: what to wear, how much money to take, what time to leave, etc. Some of these decisions are very complicated and some are quite routine in their simplicity. All, however, are very important.

1. Select destination
2. Select transportation
   2.01 Pedestrian
   2.02 Private vehicle
       2.02.01 Automobile
       2.02.02 Bicycle
   2.03 Public transportation
       2.03.01 Bus/trolley
       2.03.02 Subway
       2.03.03 Other
   2.04 Taxi
   2.05 Other
3. Select departure time
   3.01 Required arrival time
   3.02 Elapsed time required
   3.03 Conveyance timetables
       3.03.01 Single conveyance
       3.03.02 Multiple conveyance
   3.04 Other
4. Select appropriate clothing
5. Obtain funds when necessary
6. Other

T/II C: The Learner Will Follow Travel Safety Procedures

Every mode of travel has its own safety procedures: pedestrians must walk in certain locations, cross streets at certain times, etc.; automobile passengers must buckle seat belts, etc. Whatever the procedures, those who follow them have a probability of surviving longer than those who do not.

1. Follow pedestrian safety rules
   1.01 Sidewalks
   1.02 Streets
   1.03 Crossings
   1.04 Signals

2. Follow bus safety rules
   2.01 Boarding
   2.02 Sitting/standing
   2.03 Departure

3. Follow automobile safety rules
   3.01 Entering
   3.02 Sitting
   3.03 Departure

4. Other

T/II D: The Learner Will Follow Accident and Emergency Procedures

As in the other domains, situations arise in which it becomes necessary to make an emergency response. Accidents occur during travel, even on public conveyances. Consequently, it is necessary to be ready to respond if something happens.

1. Identify accident/emergency
   1.01 Accident
      1.01.01 Vehicle related
      1.01.02 Pedestrian related
      1.01.03 Other
   1.02 Injury/illness
      1.02.01 Self
      1.02.02 Other
   1.03 Travel disruptions

2. Follow accident/emergency reporting procedures
   2.01 Inform responsible person
   2.02 Local emergency telephone number
   2.03 Police/fire telephone
   2.04 Other

3. Follow accident/emergency action procedures
   3.01 Directions from responsible person
   3.02 Standard first aid procedures
   3.03 Other

4. Find alternative travel

5. Other

T/III: GOALS RELATED TO
COEXISTING WITH OTHERS
WHILE TRAVELING

Travel often brings the traveler into contact with others. As in all other social situations, saying or doing the right thing at the right time will help integrate the learner into the community. On the other hand, saying or doing the wrong things will bring negative attention and may prevent integration.

T/III A: The Learner Will Interact Appropriately With Others While Traveling

There are a number of appropriate interactions while traveling: smiling or nodding toward an approaching pedestrian when in relatively unpopulated locations (but not in heavily populated locations); asking the bus driver to announce when to get off the bus for a specific destination, etc. In addition, as is true for all other social situations, there are certain things a traveler should *not* say or do: one should not ask the bus driver the same question over and over, day after day; conversations with strangers should not go much beyond short discussions of the weather, etc., because deeply personal conversations with strangers are not usually tolerated. Low-functioning persons should learn all the skills necessary for interacting with others.

1. Perform required interactions
   1.01 Pedestrian
   1.02 Transportation officials
        1.02.01 Bus driver
        1.02.02 Automobile driver
        1.02.03 Taxi driver
        1.02.04 Information personnel
        1.02.05 Ticket sellers
        1.02.06 Other
   1.03 Fellow passengers
   1.04 Other

2. Refrain from inappropriate interactions

3. Observe demeanor constraints
   3.01 Deference
   3.02 Assertiveness
   3.03 Familiarity
   3.04 Other

4. Observe conversation restraints
   4.01 Topics
   4.02 Length
   4.03 Other

5. Exhibit appropriate body language
   5.01 Posture
   5.02 Facial expression
   5.03 Gestures
   5.04 Movements
   5.05 Other

T/III B: The Learner Will Respond Appropriately to the Inappropriate Conduct of Others While Traveling

1. Identify inappropriate conduct of others
   1.01 Aggression
      1.01.01 Physical
      1.01.02 Verbal
      1.01.03 Other
   1.02 Harassment
      1.02.01 Verbal
      1.02.02 Physical
      1.02.03 Other
   1.03 Teasing
      1.03.01 Misinformation
      1.03.02 Other
   1.04 Rudeness
   1.05 Other

2. Respond to inappropriate conduct of others
   2.01 Ignore inappropriate conduct
      2.01.01 Teasing
      2.01.02 Rudeness
   2.02 Seek assistance
      2.02.01 Aggression
      2.02.02 Harassment
      2.02.03 Other
   2.03 Avoid contact

T/IV: GOALS RELATED TO
HANDLING GLITCHES

Murphy's Law applies during travel just as much as it does in the other life domains. Equipment breaks down unexpectedly, people get lost and must seek help, injuries occur, etc. Independent travel requires the ability to respond to whatever arises.

T/IV A: The Learner Will Cope With Schedule Changes

One of the problems that can arise involves the travel schedule. For one reason or another, schedules change: a worker moves to another shift, the bus company adds or subtracts buses, etc. Whatever causes a schedule change, the traveler must adjust and cope with it.

1. Adjust when conveyance schedule changes
2. Adjust when personal routine changes
   2.01 Work schedule
   2.02 Leisure schedule
   2.03 Other
3. Inform others when unavoidable problems cause schedule changes
   3.01 Weather-imposed problems
   3.02 Personal errors
4. Other

T/IV B: The Learner Will Cope With Equipment Breakdowns During Travel

Machines are always breaking down, and sometimes so do people. When it happens, steps must be taken: alternate forms of transportation must be arranged, assistance must be found, etc.

1. Identify equipment problems
   1.01 Accident
   1.02 Breakdown
   1.03 Other

2. Respond to equipment problems
   2.01 Inform responsible person
   2.02 Identify alternate conveyance
   2.03 Other

T/IV C: The Learner Will Cope With Being Lost

Everyone loses his or her way occasionally. When it happens, it is necessary to get information about how to get to the intended destination.

1. Identify when lost
   1.01 Unknown landmarks
   1.02 Directionality

2. Respond to being lost
   2.01 Approach another person for assistance
      2.01.01 Official
      2.01.02 Nonofficial
   2.02 Follow directions to intended destination

References

Alberto, P., & Troutman, A. (1986). *Applied behavior analysis for teachers*. Columbus, OH: Merrill.

Bailey, R. (1982). *Human performance engineering*. Englewood Cliffs, NJ: Prentice-Hall.

Barker, R. (1968). *Ecological psychology: Concepts and methods for studying the environment of human behavior*. Stanford, CA: Stanford University Press.

Bloom, B. (1956). *Taxonomy of instructional objectives*. New York: David M. Kay.

Brolin, D. (Ed.) (1978). *Life centered career education: A competency based approach*. Reston, VA: Council for Exceptional Children.

Bronfenbrenner, U. (1977). Toward an experimental ecology of human development. *American Psychologist, 32*, 513–531.

Brown, L., Branston, M., Hamre-Nietupski, S., Pumpian, I., Certo, N., & Gruenewald, L. (1979). Strategy for developing age appropriate and functional curricular content for severely handicapped adolescents and young adults. *Journal of Special Education, 13*, 81–90.

Brown, L., Falvey, M., Vincent, L., Kaye, N., Johnson, F., Ferrara-Parrish, P., & Gruenewald, L. (1980). In L. Brown, M. Falvey, D. Baumgart, I. Pumpian, J. Schroeder, & L. Grunewald (Eds.), *Strategies for teaching chronological age appropriate functional skills to adolescent and young adult severely handicapped students*. Vol. IX (Part 1). Madison, WI: Madison Public Schools.

Certo, N., & Kohl, F. (1984). A strategy for developing interpersonal interaction instructional content for severely handicapped students. In N. Certo, N. Haring, & R. York (Eds.), *Public school integration of severely handicapped students*. Baltimore: Brookes.

Dever, R. (1978). *T.A.L.K. (Teaching the American Language to Kids)*. Columbus, OH: Merrill.

Dever, R. (1983). *MSH&TC curriculum*. Butlerville, IN: Muscatatuck State Hospital and Training Center.

Dever, R. (1987). *A national survey of the taxonomy of community living skills*. Bloomington, IN: Center for Innovation in Teaching the Handicapped, Working Paper 87-3.

Dewey, J. (1902). *The child and the curriculum*. Chicago: University of Chicago Press.

Donnellan, A., & Neel, R. (1986). New directions in educating sutdents with autism. In R. Horner, L. Meyer, & H. Fredericks (Eds.), *Education of learners with severe handicaps*. Baltimore: Brookes.

East Allen Public Schools (n.d.). *A manual for assessing and teaching trainable mentally retarded children*. New Haven, IN: East Allen Schools.

Easterday, J., & Sitlington, P. (1985). *Conducting an analysis of community work environments relative to employment of the severely handicapped*. Bloomington, IN: Center for Innovation in Teaching the Handicapped.

Falvey, M. (1986). *Community-based curriculum: Educational strategies for students with severe handicaps*. Baltimore: Brookes.

Ford, A., Brown, L., Pumpian, I., Baumgart, D., Nisbet, J., Schroeder, J., & Loomis, R. (1984). Strategies for developing individualized recreation and leisure programs for severely handicapped students. In N. Certo, N. Haring, & R. York (Eds.), *Public school integration of severely handicapped students*. Baltimore: Brookes.

Gay, G. (1980). Conceptual models of the curriculum planning process. In A Foshay (Ed.), *Considered action for curriculum improvement*, Alexandria, VA: Association for Supervision and Curriculum Development.

Gaylord-Ross, R., & Holvoet, J. (1985). *Strategies for educating students with severe handicaps*. Boston: Little-Brown.

Gold, M. (1980). *Did I say that?* Champaign, IL: Research Press.

Grossman, H. J. (1973). *Manual on terminology and classification in mental retardation*. Washington, DC: American Association on Mental Deficiency.

Grossman, H. J. (1983). *Manual on terminology and classification in mental retardation*. Washington, DC: American Association on Mental Deficiency.

Guess, D. (1980). Methods in communication instruction for severely handicapped persons. In W. Sailor, B. Wilcox, & L. Brown (Eds.), *Methods of instruction for severely handicapped students*. Baltimore: Brookes.

Guess, D., & Helmstetter, E. (1986). Skill cluster instruction and the individualized curriculum sequencing model. In R. Horner, L. Meyer, & H. Fredericks (Eds.), *Education of learners with severe handicaps*. Baltimore: Brookes.

Guess, D., Horner, R., Utley, B., Holvoet, J., Maxon, D., Tucker, D., & Warren, S. (1978). A functional curriculum sequencing model for teaching the severely handicapped. *AAESPH Review, 3*, 201–215.

Guess, D., Sailor, W., & Baer, D. (1976). *Functional speech and language training*. Austin: Pro-Ed.

Gunzburg, H.C. (1973). *Progress assessment chart*. 6th Edition. Birmingham, ENG: SEFA Ltd.

Halpern, A. (1985). Transition: A look at foundations. *Exceptional Children, 51*, 479–486.

Haring, N. G. (1977a). *Developing effective individualized educational programs for severely handicapped children and youth*. Washington, DC: Bureau for the Education of the Handicapped, HEW.

Haring, N. G. (1977b). *From promise to reality. AAESPH Review, 1* 3–7.

Heber, R. (1962). *A manual on terminology and classification in mental retardation*. Washington, DC: American Association on Mental Deficiency.

Horner, R., McDonnell, J., & Bellamy, G. (1986). Teaching general case skills: General case instruction in simulation and communication settings. In R. Horner, L. Meyer, & H. Fredricks (Eds.), *Education of learners with severe handicaps*. Baltimore: Brookes.

Horner, R., Meyer, L., & Fredericks, H. (1986). *Education of learners with severe handicaps*. Baltimore: Brookes.

Horner, R., Sprague, J., & Wilcox, B. (1982). General case programming for community activities. In B. Wilcox & G. Bellamy (Eds.), *Design of high school programs for severely handicapped students*. Baltimore: Brookes.

Knapczyk, D. (1983). Use of teacher paced instruction in developing and maintaining independent self-feeding. *Journal of the Association for Persons with Severe Handicaps, 8*, 10–17.

Knapczyk, D., Johnson, W., & McDermott, G. (1983). A comparison of the effects of teacher and peer supervision on work performance and on-task behavior. *Journal of the Association for Persons with Severe Handicaps, 8*, 41–49.

Kokaska, C. J., & Brolin, E.D. (1986). *Career education for handicapped individuals*. 2nd Edition. Columbus, OH: Merrill.

Lakin, C., & Bruininks, R. (1985). Social integration of developmentally disabled persons. In C. Lakin & R. Bruininks (Eds.), *Strategies for achieving community integration of developmentally disabled citizens*. Baltimore: Brookes.

Liberty, K. (1985). Enhancing instruction for maintenance, generalization, and adaptation. In C. Lakin & R. Bruininks (Eds.), *Strategies for achieving community integration of developmentally disabled citizens*. Baltimore: Brookes.

MacDonald, J., & Horstmeier, D. (1978). *Environmental language intervention program*. Columbus, OH: Merrill.

Mager, R. (1962). *Preparing instructional objectives*. San Francisco: Fearon.

Meyer, L., & Evans, I. (1986). Modification of excess behavior: An adaptive and functional approach for educational and community contexts. In R. Horner, L. Meyer, & H. Fredericks (Eds.), *Education of learners with severe handicaps*. Baltimore: Brookes.

Mook, D. (1987). *Motivation: The organization of action*. New York: Norton.

Moon, S., Goodall, P., Barcus, M., & Brooke, V. (1985). *The supported work model of competitive employment for citizens with severe handicaps*. Richmond, VA: Virginia Commonwealth University.

Nietupski, Jr., Hamre-Nietupski, S., Clancy, P., & Veerhusen, K. (1986). Guidelines for making simluation an effective adjunct to in vivo community instruction. *Journal of the Association for Persons with Severe Handicaps, 8*, 3–15.

Patton, J., Payne, J., & Bierne-Smith, M. (1986). *Mental retardation*. Columbus, OH: Merrill.

Popham, W., & Baker, E. (1970). *Systematic instruction*. Englewood Cliffs, NJ: Prentice-Hall.

Popovich, D., & Laham, S. (Eds.). (1981). *The adaptive behavior curriculum: Prescriptive behavior analysis for moderately, severely, and profoundly handicapped students*. Mt. Clemens, MI: Macomb School District.

Reichle, J., & Keogh, W. (1986). Communication instruction for learners with severe handicaps. In R. Horner, L. Meyer, & H. Fredericks (Eds.), *Education of learners with severe handicaps.* Baltimore: Brookes.

Rusch, F., Chadsey-Rusch, J., & Lagomarcino, T. (1987). Preparing students for employment. In M. Snell (Ed.), *Systematic instruction for persons with severe handicaps.* Columbus, OH: Merrill.

Rusch, F., & Mithaug, D. (1985). Competitive employment education. In C. Lakin & R. Bruininks (Eds.), *Strategies for achieving community integration of developmentally disabled citizens.* Baltimore: Brookes.

Sailor, W. (1975). The TARC system: Instructional objectives for the severely handicapped. *AAESPH Review, 1,* 1–13.

Sailor, W., & Guess, D. (1983). *Severely handicapped students: An instructional design.* Boston: Houghton-Mifflin.

Sailor, W., Halvorson, A., Anderson, J., Goetz, L., Gee, K., Doering, K., & Hunt, P. (1986). Community intensive instruction. In R. Horner, L. Meyer, & H. Fredericks (Eds.), *Education of learners with severe handicaps.* Baltimore: Brookes.

Sarason, S. B., & Doris, J. (1969). *Psychological problems in mental deficiency.* 4th Edition. New York: Harper & Row.

Scheerenberger, R. C. (1983). *A history of mental retardation.* New York: Wiley.

Schultz, R., Williams, W., Iverson, G., & Duncan, D. (1984). Social integration of severely handicapped students. In N. Certo, N. Haring, & R. York (Eds.), *Public school integration of severely handicapped students.* Baltimore: Brookes.

Smith, B. O., Stanley, W. O., & Shores, B. H. (1957). *Fundamentals of curriculum development.* Yonkers: World Book.

Snell, M. (1987). *Systematic instruction of persons with severe handicaps.* Columbus, OH: Merrill.

Snell, M., & Browder, D. (1986). Community-referenced instruction: Research issues. *Journal of the Association for Persons with Severe Handicaps, 11,* 1–11.

Snell, M., & Smith, D. (1987). Developing the IEP: Selecting and assessing skills. In M. Snell (Ed.), *Systematic instruction of the moderately and severely handicapped.* Columbus, OH: Merrill.

Taba, H. (1962). *Curriculum development: Theory and practice.* New York: Harcourt, Brace Javonivich.

Tanner, D., & Tanner, L. (1980). *Curriculum development: Theory into Practice.* 2nd Edition. New York: MacMillan.

Taylor, V., Close, D., Carlson, C., & Larrabee, D. (1981). *Independent living skills curriculum.* Eugene, OR: University of Oregon.

Tuckman, B., & Edwards, K. (1971). A systems model for instructional design and management. *Educational Technology 11,* 21–26.

Tyler, R. W. (1957). The curriculum—then and now. *Proceedings of the 1956 Invitational Conference on Testing Problems.* Princeton, NJ: Educational Testing Service.

Vash, C. L. (1977). *Sheltered industrial employment: Emerging issues in rehabilitation.* Washington, DC: Rehabilitation Services Administration.

Vocational Opportunities Cooperative. (1982). *VOCSKILLS.* New Berlin, WI: Ideal Development Labs.

Vogelsburg, R. T., Anderson, J., Berger, P., Haselden, T., Mitwell, S., Schmidt, C., Skowron, A., Ulett, D., & Wilcox, B. (1980). Programming for apartment living: A description and rationale for an independent living skills inventory. *Journal of the Association for the Severely Handicapped, 5,* (1), 38–54.

Wacker, D., & Hoffman, R. (1984). Severely and profoundly mentally retarded students. In P. Valletutti & B. Sims-Tucker (Eds.), *Severely and profoundly handicapped students.* Baltimore: Brookes.

Wehman, P., Kregel, J., & Barcus, J. (1985). From school to work: A vocational transition model for handicapped students. *Exceptional Children, 52,* 25–37.

Wessel, J. (1976). *I can program.* Northbrook, IL: Hubbard Scientific.

White, O. (1980). Adaptive performance objectives: Form vs. function. In W. Sailor, B. Wilcox, & L. Brown (Eds.), *Methods of instruction for severely handicapped students.* Baltimore: Brookes.

Wilcox, B. & Bellamy, G. (1982). *Design of high school programs for severely handicapped students.* Baltimore: Brookes.

Will, M. (1984). *Programming for the transition of youth with disabilities: Bridges from school to working life.* Washington, DC: Office of Special Education and Rehabilitation Services.

Zais, R. (1976). *Curriculum: Principles and foundations.* New York: Crowell.

Index